Paul M. W. Hackett • Jessica B. Schwarzenbach •
Uta Maria Jürgens
Consumer Psychology: A Study Guide to
Qualitative Research Methods

Paul M. W. Hackett
Jessica B. Schwarzenbach
Uta Maria Jürgens

Consumer Psychology: A Study Guide to Qualitative Research Methods

Barbara Budrich Publishers
Opladen • Berlin • Toronto 2016

A CIP catalogue record for this book is available from
Die Deutsche Bibliothek (The German Library)

© 2016 by Barbara Budrich Publishers, Opladen, Berlin & Toronto
        www.barbara-budrich.net

ISBN   978-3-8474-0772-0
eISBN   978-3-8474-0891-8

Das Werk einschließlich aller seiner Teile ist urheberrechtlich geschützt. Jede Verwertung außerhalb der engen Grenzen des Urheberrechtsgesetzes ist ohne Zustimmung des Verlages unzulässig und strafbar. Das gilt insbesondere für Vervielfältigungen, Übersetzungen, Mikroverfilmungen und die Einspeicherung und Verarbeitung in elektronischen Systemen.

Die Deutsche Bibliothek – CIP-Einheitsaufnahme
Ein Titeldatensatz für die Publikation ist bei der Deutschen Bibliothek erhältlich.

Verlag Barbara Budrich ⒷⒷ Barbara Budrich Publishers
Stauffenbergstr. 7. D-51379 Leverkusen Opladen, Germany

86 Delma Drive. Toronto, ON M8W 4P6 Canada
www.barbara-budrich.net

Jacket illustration by disegno, Wuppertal, Germany –
        disegno-kommunikation.de
Picture credits: © Slavomir Valigursky/Fotolia.com
Typesetting: Judith Henning, Hamburg, Germany – www.buchfinken.com
Editing: Alison Romer, Lancaster, UK
Printed in Europe on acid-free paper by paper&tinta, Warsaw, Poland

Book Sections

Detailed table of contents

List of Figures

List of Tables

Preface

This study guide constitutes a concise guide aimed to assist you, a higher-level undergraduate student who has little or no previous research experience. It forms an outline of a course in qualitative research methods in consumer psychology. The text is practical rather than theoretical. The qualitative (non-numerical) research methodologies that we, the authors, present comprise what we believe to be a representative set of methods that may be used to investigate consumer behaviour in a qualitative manner. Moreover, to familiarize you with the structure of a scientific report and assist you with making sense of the complexities of research articles as well as the practical writing and presenting of your own investigations, we offer specific details about how to construct, write, and present a research study.

The study guide emphasises the benefits of working together in teams, not only to facilitate cooperation, but also to encourage insight amongst students of varied skills when addressing applied consumer investigative questions. Although teamwork will often be mentioned in the text, you will be able to undertake all procedures as an individual investigator.

As a unique addition to this discussion of research methods, we have introduced a model of a course which can be assessed through a group project that runs throughout an entire semester and involves students carrying-out the approaches to consumer behaviour research that are discussed in the guide. In addition to details of the group project, individual assignments and other integrated tasks are also presented. The group research project, central to the course, incorporates a series of individual research activities and involves designing, conducting, and analysing a qualitative and ethnographic study of a product or service within the context of a college setting.

This guide, then, provides you with an introduction to 10 approaches to qualitative consumer psychology research. When the material in this text is incorporated with the sample course model, students will not only experience, but also be able to demonstrate an in-depth knowledge of qualitative methods applicable to consumer psychology. All course and writing guidelines are open to modification, as each instructor will have his or her own unique perspective on the presentation of the materials. It is important, however, that you realize books do not provide an alternative to attending lectures nor to participating in research procedures as an individual or active member of a research team. In this guide, we help you build a bridge between theory and practice of consumer research: We assist you in devising a "sample" research project, i.e. a mental model for an actual research project about a product or service that you can either choose to actually realize as part of a course, or to just help you think through the research approaches we present here.

Synopsis of Chapters

In section one of this study guide, Planning the Research Project, there are three chapters that offer information about the nature of qualitative consumer research and how you might plan your own research investigations. In chapter one, definitions of qualitative consumer research and consumer ethnography are suggested. In the second chapter the mapping sentence is introduced as a tool that you may use to manage your consumer research project and to design the framework for writing-up your research report and final presentation. In chapter three, a brief account of the development of ethical practice associated with research that employs human subjects is offered. Great emphasis is placed upon the need to act ethically in all research situations.

In section two, Approaches to Qualitative Research Methods in Consumer Psychological Research, you will be introduced to research procedures. The chapters in this section are as follows: Chapter four – Projective Techniques; Chapter five – Focus Groups; Chapter six – In-Depth Interviews; Chapter seven – Ethnography; Chapter eight – Netnography; Chapter nine – Artefact Research; Chapter ten – Archival Research; Chapter eleven – Journals and Diaries; and Chapter twelve – Autoethnography. In this section each of these qualitative research approaches are described with each chapter following a similar structure: first details of a specific technique are given; then a reply to the query, "What Questions Does This Technique Answer?" is provided. Next an understanding of the Limitations of the Approach (Practical Limitations, Cost Limitations and Bias Limitations) is offered for each method. Each of these chapters contains a "Now You" section that provides you with some food for thought about the respective methods and thus helps you familiarize yourself with the idea of this approach. Finally, a comprehensive list of Further Reading is included at the end of each of these chapters in order to invite you, as an interested student or course designer, to expand your exploration of the many perspectives of qualitative research.

In section three, Practical Procedures, details are provided as to how you, as an individual researcher or as a member of a research team, might undertake each of the procedures listed in section two. Each research approach will be considered in the order in which it was presented in section two and each chapter will be structured to answer the typical questions you will have to consider while conducting the research. Next, we provide you with the information as to what you will have to do in preparation for undertaking the procedure. There follows a series of passages in which information is given about: the research location (where we suggest you undertake the procedure); the materials that are necessary to conduct the research; the participants; a full review of the research procedure; an outline of the type of results that might be expected to arise; and finally, specific analyses that are appropriate for each of the procedures.

In section 4, we furnish an explicit account of how to analyse the data from a research project and how to write up your own investigation.

In the appendices full details are given of a prototypic course of study in qualitative consumer research, including particulars of the schedule students might be expected to undergo during this type of study. Also included in the appendices is a list of the chapters from *Qualitative Methods in Consumer Psychology: Ethnography and Culture* (Paul Hackett (2015), London: Routledge), which provides in-depth information on each methodology described in this work.

The study guide is a comprehensive text that is designed to enhance your understanding of qualitative methods if you are a student, as well as assisting you with the development of creative courses in consumer research, if you are a teacher or curriculum designer.

Section 1 – Planning the Research Project

Chapter 1. What are Qualitative Research Methods in Qualitative Consumer Psychological Research?

This study guide places emphasis upon qualitative consumer psychological research approaches and procedures including ethnographic and cultural analyses. Consumer psychology may be defined as the application of psychological principles and knowledge to understand consumers (this includes clients, users, buyers, customers, et cetera) in terms of their attitudes, beliefs, values, memories, etc., and how these are intertwined with and reciprocally influence their commercially related behaviours. Within the context of this book the adoption of psychological approaches implies that the researcher will attempt to maintain an analytical perspective and will keep exemplary documentation when conducting consumer behaviour research. Qualitative research in consumer psychology typically gathers non-number-based and non-statistical information about consumers and concerns itself with data collected from narrative types of sources. Consumer ethnography is the application of research approaches, which attempt to develop understanding of consumers' cultural behaviours and experiences.

Ethnography may itself be briefly defined as a form of research that involves gathering data from, and developing understanding about, people through involvement with those people, and in a variety of ways, assembling rich information about their lives. Furthermore, ethnography is almost exclusively concerned with the collection of in-depth, verbal and observational information, which is heavily reliant upon personal accounts and narratives rather than numerical information. On its most traditional definition, ethnography involves the trained researcher (usually an anthropologist) in becoming an active member, or participant observer, of a culture for a period of a year or so. Because of the cost of conducting research over such a protracted time period and the competitive urgency of consumer research, the length of consumer ethnographic research projects have been truncated and participant observation has been supplemented with a variety of other qualitative research approaches.

Cultural analysis is the investigation of the influence of cultures and subcultures on consumers. Different methodologies will be suggested to encourage understanding of various aspects of the impact of culture on individuals and social groups in terms of decision-making and marketing communication campaigns.

The approaches to undertaking research that are presented in this text are selected from those that are typically found in marketing and allied fields which employ what are usually termed qualitative, ethnographic, and cultural perspectives. This book creates a template for an applied course. We encourage you, our readers, to choose a sample research project to conduct, with which you may tentatively employ most of the qualitative procedures covered in this guide. Even though learning works best through practice, we understand that not all readers have the time and resources to actually conduct this type of research project. However, we recommend that you actively think through the approaches presented here with respect to your chosen sample project in a way *as if* you wanted to actually realize a study. To this end, think about a product or service that you are interested in, i.e. about which you would want to learn more from the perspective of a researcher who looks at consumers' responses to that product or service. The object of research can be anything from the veggie meal in the cafeteria to a new sports car or a special cut-and-go offer of a local coiffeur. In this text, we will stress the practical considerations that need to be scrutinized when designing and conducting qualitative marketing research. You will get the most out of the study guide when you apply these considerations to your sample project. We will support this semi-applied learning process with detailed suggestions throughout the text.

The Research Cycle

The authors place significance upon the notion that research takes a cyclical approach to asking questions and finding answers. Figure 1 below illustrates the circular nature of the research process:

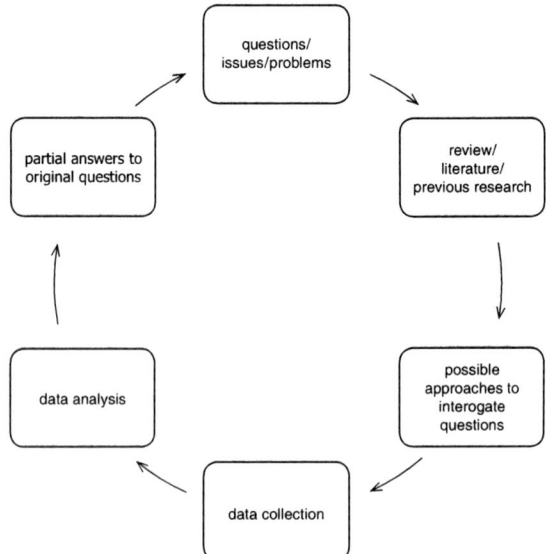

Figure 1. Research Cycle

When attempting to understand the diagram above, the reader enters the cyclic process at the 'questions, issues, problems' stage at the top of the diagram. Here the researcher decides which questions, issues or problems are of concern to his or her research. During this phase in the project the researcher essentially makes concrete his or her questions and delimits the scope of the research to be conducted.

The researcher then follows the path of the arrows to the right and down to the next stage in the research cycle. Here the researcher seeks and then evaluates background information about the product or service of interest. The researcher investigates other studies that have been undertaken into similar services or products or any other information that exists that can usefully be used to inform the design and analysis of the current research project. This stage should start by looking widely and gathering a comprehensive range of information, which should then be sorted through until only the most pertinent information remains.

Stage three of the research cycle is another process involving the searching for and evaluation of research possibilities. However, at this stage the researcher is not looking for background information about the product or service but asking questions about what will be the most appropriate research approaches to use. The answer to these inquiries will come from the personal experiences and training of the researcher(s) and also from similar research that has been published in the literature.

Having made the decisions that are inherent in the first three stages of the research cycle, the researcher actually gathers data in stage 4. It is important to stress that each of the stages in the research cycle, and especially during the data gathering stage, are not as simple as the book seems to indicate. Some of the intricacies involved in actually progressing through the research cycle will be considered later in the text. In stage 5 the data that has been gathered is now analysed appropriately. This action leads to stage 6 in which answers are provided to the questions that were initially stated in stage 1.

In figure 1, stage 6 is represented through the verbal description "partial answers." Unless the research topic and its questions are exceptionally simple, the answers produced in stage 6 will inevitably be partial and new questions will also arise from the research. Thus, with the partial answers in mind, along with the new questions suggested by the research, the researcher re-enters, or another researcher enters, the research cycle at stage 1 with a modified question(s). From this point the researcher again progresses around the research cycle and with each cycle the research becomes fuller and more useable.

The Research Project: Five Practical Considerations

Now, it is time for you to think about a (sample) research project – either a project that you will actually conduct as part of a course in qualitative consumer research, or a sample project that will be your mental template to think through the research procedures presented here. Begin by thinking about a product or service that is interesting to you. What would you want to learn more about in terms of consumers' reactions to, interactions with, or usage of your product or service? How could consumers' relationships be improved with your product, etc.? From this first idea you will develop, step-by-step, your research plan, i.e. a road map for entering and then completing the research circle presented in figure 1.

At the early stages of a research project it is important to ask questions about the feasibility of your proposed research plan. Therefore, in an attempt to weigh the practical and sensible possibilities of any research project you should ask the five questions shown in figure 2. These are simple and realistic questions that may be easily overlooked when you are excited about a potential research topic that you would like to investigate. However, without asking these questions you may take on a research project that you will have difficulty completing. The five questions are given in figure 2 and they culminate in the general question that the researcher or research team should carefully consider: 'Can I (we) do this research project'?

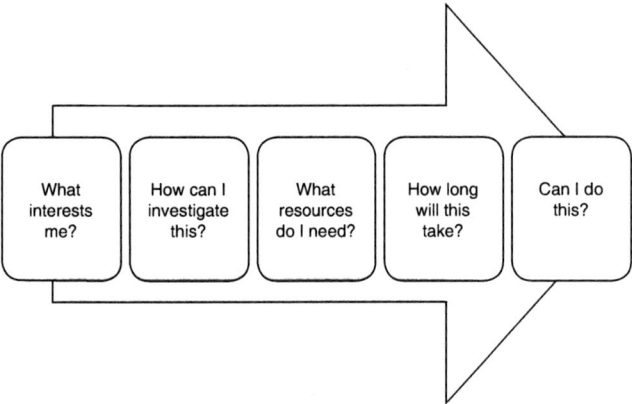

Figure 2. Practical Research Considerations

The Three Essential Aspects of Useful Research

Thus far we have considered the cyclic nature of undertaking a research project and assessing the feasibilities of conducting a research project. However, other questions must be asked about whether the findings of a research project are likely to be of practical use. In this study guide we claim that for a research project to yield useful information it must meet the three criteria of being: ethical, valid (trustworthy) and reliable (see figure 3).

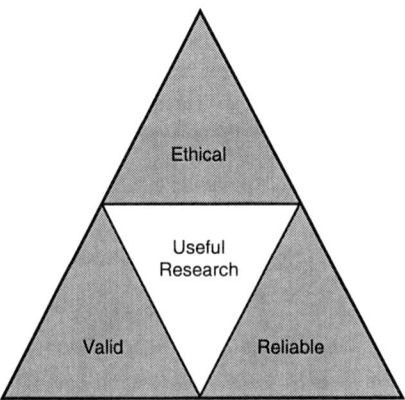

Figure 3. Three Components of Useful Research

Ethicality

There are many aspects of ethics within marketing research and many of these will be considered in this text. However, in summary, research ethics can be seen to include: the minimization of harm to participants; the equitable distribution of risk and benefits between participants and research sponsors associated with the research; the use of the best, least costly, least potentially dangerous research approach possible; the conservation of researcher integrity and honesty; the obtainment of informed written consent from participants; the preservation of participant anonymity/confidentiality; and always respecting participants as well as informing and allowing participant withdrawal at any time at no cost to them.

When working within institutions (especially schools, universities, and colleges) research generally needs to be presented to an Institutional Review Board (IRB) for approval before it is commenced. The IRB evaluates the ethical nature of the proposed study and makes a judgment as to whether the project shows due respect to those involved, is financially and temporally feasible and to be conducted by persons with appropriate qualifications. The Board also ensures that the investigator provides suitable consent forms for the specific project. Sometimes the research is exempt from the IRB's examination, i.e., such as when human subjects are to be drawn from students participating in a research methods class. Yet more likely than not, researchers working under college authority must obtain informed written consent from all human subjects who participate in their studies. Ethical considerations are interspersed throughout the Study Guide and are discussed in greater depth in chapter 3.

In order for students to better understand the ethical requirements of conducting research with human subjects, we suggest that a course include an institutional review board application as part of the student research project. Students in the US may also be asked to complete a short NIH (National Institutes of Health) approved online course in ethical competence.

Validity/trustworthiness

When speaking about the validity of any qualitative research, including qualitative consumer psychology research, we are considering the extent to which the research is producing correct, trustworthy and valuable answers. There are different forms of validity that might be considered, but specifically, a research project is seen to be valid if it is talking about the phenomena it is claiming to be talking about. Establishing validity and trustworthiness in a research project is an attempt to reduce bias in the results of qualitative research.

Reliability

Reliability also attempts to reduce bias in qualitative research and is concerned with the ability of your research to produce roughly similar results if the context in which the data is gathered and the procedures used in the research, etc., remain constant. Various types of research reliability ought to be considered in any introduction to qualitative research methods.

Three Components of Useful Research

In all cases, whatever type of research you undertake or approach you choose, there are three essential questions that you must ask yourself when attempting to establish the quality, strengths and limitations of the research you are viewing or when you are designing a research project:

1/ How ethical is this research?
2/ How valid or trustworthy is this research?
3/ How reliable is this research?

Take some time to think through what ethicality, validity and reliability might mean with regard to your speculative or actual research project. Who might be harmed or embarrassed by the research? How can you make sure your research actually addresses the concepts in which you are interested? What could be obstacles in reproducing the results of your research? The details we provide on the questions of ethicality, validity and reliability in further chapters will help you to hone your sample research plan.

Research Methods, Philosophies and Approaches

There are many methods for conducting qualitative research within the context of consumer psychology. This guide introduces several of these as well as a variety of different theoretical perspectives, research designs, and ways to analyse data that come out of a research project. Some of these possible choices are listed in figure 4:

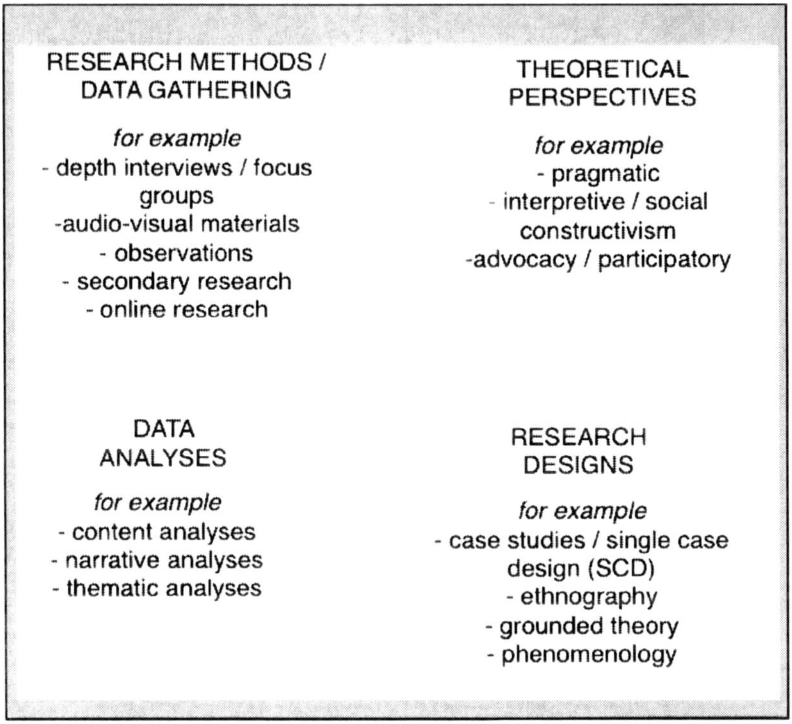

RESEARCH METHODS / DATA GATHERING	THEORETICAL PERSPECTIVES
for example - depth interviews / focus groups -audio-visual materials - observations - secondary research - online research	*for example* - pragmatic - interpretive / social constructivism -advocacy / participatory
DATA ANALYSES	RESEARCH DESIGNS
for example - content analyses - narrative analyses - thematic analyses	*for example* - case studies / single case design (SCD) - ethnography - grounded theory - phenomenology

Figure 4. Research Methods: Approaches and Perspectives

Looking at figure 4 you can see that choices exist at all stages of conducting a qualitative consumer research project. For example, a specific theoretical perspective underpins each of the possible qualitative research methods that may be adopted. Figure 4 demonstrates that these theoretical perspectives may include, but are not limited to: pragmatic; interpretive/social constructivist; advocacy/participatory. The adoption of a theoretical perspective will heavily influence the ways in which you will conduct research, the types of data you will consider to be most useful, and the ways in which you will gather and analyse your data. What figure 4 demonstrates is that there are many choices (those shown in figure 4 are but a few from many more possibilities) that a researcher may make at all stages of research inquiry and that choices made at one stage will have an influence at other stages and upon the overall project.

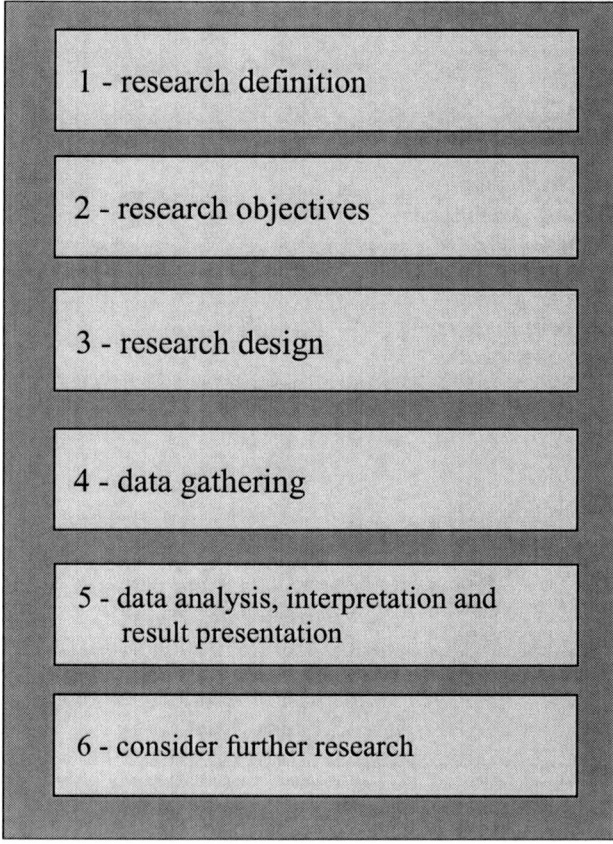

Figure 5. The Research Process

The diagram above provides a framework to guide you through the research process in a clear and unambiguous manner and supplies a template for the effective writing-up of a research project. Table 1 below demonstrates the correspondence between the research cycle and the research process.

Table 1 Research Cycle and Components of the Research Process

Stage Phase	Research cycle	Components of research process
1	Questions/issues/problems	Define research goal
2	Review literature/previous research	Define research objectives given what is already known
3	Possible approaches to interrogate questions	Compose design: Define and explain methodology
4	Data collection	Gather data
5	Data analysis	Analyse data and interpret results
6	Partial answers	Discuss in which way results answer questions and if further research is needed

Earlier a cyclic structure for the research process (see figure 1) was introduced. The research cycle represents how research progresses in the real world. However, when actively planning and writing a research paper it may be more useful to think of this cyclic nature of research as also being a linear procedure: the true cyclic aspect of the research process may then be considered after the results of the research have been documented. By thinking of the research write-up as a linear activity, you may have an easier time staying focused upon the actual findings of the current research. Later in preparing the research report, i.e. after the full account of the present research has been made, you will need to consider alterations and improvements to the procedure. Having made changes you may then return to the first research step and enter into another round of the research cycle with further projects.

Chapter 2. Using a Mapping Sentence to Manage a Consumer Research Project

Introduction

In this chapter the importance of organizing your research project is stressed. A clear and explicit structure will help you achieve you research aims in a timely fashion. A straightforward plan will also enable you to unambiguously investigate the key aspects of your research and to better integrate the findings from numerous research techniques: We suggest using a project-management mapping sentence[1] to help you build such a structure.

A project-management mapping sentence provides a definitional system to organize the content of an investigation in a manner that assists you to better understand the complex inter-relations of data. The mapping sentence specifies who or what will be investigated, the types of data that will be gathered, and the research approaches to be used. Together, these elements form the management plan and a template for data analysis.

How does a mapping sentence assist with research?

Many aspects of the ethnographic research project must be kept in mind when attempting to understand and conduct qualitative consumer investigations. For example, the research questions in a project originate from experience or literature as do hypotheses, or informed conjectures. These questions and hypotheses, along with the literature you view, may significantly influence the answers your study produces. For example, your questions and hypotheses will effect:

1/   The types of data gathered to answer these enquiries
2/   How the data is analysed
3/   The types of answers produced by the research
4/   The inferences that may be made based upon your findings

Therefore, clearly understanding the questions that are being asked in each component of your research project is of great importance. The mapping sentence will help you to design questions and all other aspects of the research project.

Research planning is a vital and often ignored aspect of behavioural research. Indeed, the first author has attended research classes over many

---

1   The mapping sentence is a tool from the general approach to social research known as facet theory, which will be briefly mentioned as necessary.

years in a variety of disciplines at all levels of tertiary education but is unable to recall attending a class that addressed research planning or research program management. Qualitative research often produces copious amounts of data of a wide variety of types (from visual images to narrative texts). Because of the different techniques that may be used to analyse these disparate data forms, the project may become large, convoluted, and in other ways messy. Therefore planning and careful management is needed in order to:

1/ Attain research goals
2/ Remain clearly focused upon the research questions
3/ Stay within time schedules
4/ Manage multiple researchers in a research team
5/ Coordinate the timing of the different research approaches or sub-projects that may be used in your study

Within all of these intricate components research projects need purposeful management. The mapping sentence is the major research tool used in research within the rubric of facet theory. Facet theory is an approach to social research that looks for meaning in the concepts being studied. This process or meta-theory (theory about a theory) was conceived in the middle of the last century by Louis Guttman and has been used by social scientists to investigate complex social behaviour within many contexts. The mapping sentence provides a structure within which a research domain, and the data that is gathered to investigate this domain, can be understood. Structure in facet theory research refers to the formal arrangement within a mapping sentence of research questions, respondents, background features of the research, research variables along with hypotheses for the inclusion of these components.

What is a mapping sentence?

In greater detail, a mapping sentence that is used to manage a research project is made up of three types or categories of information (these categories are called facets). The three types of facet are the background facet, the content facet, and the range facet. We will now consider each of these facets.

Within the mapping sentence **background facets** specify details of the events, people, or objects to be classified and/or investigated in the research project. Background facets may also be segments of the user population who you believe to be important in understanding how customers relate to your product (e.g., segments of: age; gender; owner or non-owner of the product).

Content facets specify how a research domain will be investigated in the project. Content facets identify the specific research techniques that you will be using (focus group, in-depth interview, netnography, etc.). If you have a

28

research project with one research approach (say, just an IDI), then there will be a single content facet in the mapping sentence. More complex designs will have a greater number of content facets. Each of these facets will have a series of appropriate elements that list the format of data that each technique is designed to yield (e.g., IDI: deep and reflective emotional reactions – thoughts – and reports about behaviours; Netnography: typical and unusual reactions to a product within an online forum, etc.).

The **range facet**[2] specifies the overall orientation of the research project (e.g., overall customer satisfaction)[3].

Thus to recap, when a mapping sentence is used as a research management technique, it becomes a formal statement of the procedures that will be undertaken to examine the research project's question(s). Each procedure is stated as a content facet in the mapping sentence. For each of these types of procedural facets, the expected form of information that will be yielded through using this procedure is stated in terms of a content facet's elements. Each of these content facets are linked to each other using connecting words to form a sentence with a structure that approximates normal prose. The sentence suggests the expected inter-relationship between the content facets within the context of the specific research project.

In figure 6 below we provide an example of a project-management mapping sentence that is used to design and oversee a study investigating consumers' satisfaction with modifications to the design of an automobile. Prior to the specification of the content facets in a mapping sentence, background facets are usually stated to provide the context to the mapping sentence. Background facets are the characteristic of the respondents in a study or aspects of the research situation that the researcher believes to be related to consumers' attitudes and behaviours towards the product of interest. For example, in a study to assess users reactions to modifications in the design of an automobile, background facets may include: gender; whether the participant is an owner of this model of car or not; whether the participant was sitting in the car or in their own homes when they were completing the questionnaire; etc.

---

2 The range facet is usually but not always present in a project-management-mapping sentence.

3 The above listed facets are abstract at present but we will later bring sense to these terms with some appropriate examples.

<pre>
                         gender   ownership
Person (x) being: (male   )   who previously has: (owned   )
                         (female)   (not owned)

                                                             IDI
the model of automobile being investigated, revealed his/her deep: (emotions   )
                                                             (thoughts   )
                                                             (behaviours)

                                                             FGI
during IDIs in relation to the automobile, and offered: (innovations)   during
                                                             (warnings   )
                                                             (beliefs   )

focus group interviews, and demonstrated her/his interactions with the automobile to be:

ethnography
(typical   )   observed forms of behaviour, that suggests that she/he is:
(unusual   )
(emergency)

    range
(highly satisfied   )   with the overall design changes to the automobile.
(to   )
(highly dissatisfied)
</pre>

Figure 6. Mapping Sentence for Customer Satisfaction with Automobile Design[4]

In the above example, the elements of the gender facet can either be male or female whilst the ownership facet can be either a previous owner or not a previous owner of the automobile model being investigated (other elements are of course possible for each of these facets but for the sake of this example the suggested elements will suffice). Furthermore, there could have been a greater or fewer number of background facets. Indeed there could have been none at all if no background characteristics of respondents, products, services, location of the research, etc., were thought to meaningfully impact upon the outcome of the overall research project.

Reading the mapping sentence from left to right as you would an ordinary sentence, you encounter the content facets after the background facets. In this sentence the content facets specified are: In-Depth Interview (IDI); Focus Group Interview (FGI); Ethnography. A greater or smaller number of

---

4   IDI = In Depth Interview, FGI = Focus Group Interview

research procedures may be incorporated; as content facets within a project planning mapping sentence are dependent upon the number of procedures used in the research project. Each of the content facets has their respective elements specified. The elements state the *type* of information that is expected to arise from the procedure. For example, IDIs are expected to produce responses that may be discretely identified as being about respondents: deep thoughts; feelings; or actions towards or about the automobile. The focus group interview has elements that again are relatively discrete but in this procedure they are expected to have a content that may be typified as innovatory statements, the providing of warnings or belief related comments. Finally, the Ethnography facet has two discrete elements that categorise observed behaviours that are related to automobiles as being either: typical behaviours or unusual behaviours.

After choosing the content facets in a mapping sentence, an expected range for the overall project is stated. The range in a project planning mapping sentence consists of the overall consumer reaction or behaviour that the entirety of your research project is attempting to assess. For example, the overall aim of the above research project is to assess users' satisfaction with modifications to an automobile's design and the range facet for this research project would range from highly satisfied to highly dissatisfied. The elements in this range facet are continuous and demonstrate how a person may occupy a subtly differentiated position from being highly satisfied to highly dissatisfied with the automobile's design.

This mapping sentence, as with all mapping sentences, is viewed as if it were a normal sentence of prose with a single facet element from each of the content facets being included each time the mapping sentence is read. The sentence will be read through several times and each reading will incorporate different facet element combinations. For example, one reading may be:

Person (x) being: female who previously has *not owned* the model of automobile being investigated, revealed her deep *emotions* during IDIs in relation to the automobile, offered *beliefs* during focus group interviews, and demonstrated her interactions with the automobile to be *unusual* observed forms of behaviour, all of which suggest the participant to be *dissatisfied* with the overall design changes to the automobile.

Another reading of the mapping sentence with different elements chosen from each facet may be:

Person (x) being: male who previously has *owned* the model of automobile being investigated revealed his deep *thoughts* during IDIs in relation to the automobile, offered *warnings* during focus group interviews and demonstrated his interactions with the automobile to be **typical** observed forms of behaviour, all of which suggest the participant to be *very satisfied* with the overall design changes to the automobile.

Try to devise such a mapping sentence that sketches your research project! Use Figure 6 as a template and create the facets for your research accordingly.

Why do I need to plan and manage a research project?

By its very nature, research is complicated as investigators are attempting to make inquiries about things that interest them and to find explanations for what they observe. In qualitative consumer research a project may employ several different approaches to investigating the question of interest and can include, for example, interviews, focus groups, observations, and digitally based research all within the same project. This complexity requires careful and explicit planning for proper management of the study[5].

To illustrate this complexity let us take a hypothetical example. When a researcher is investigating a specific product, let's say a new beverage for sale in a local café, the vendor will be interested in the customers' reactions to the beverage itself: it's taste, aroma, appearance, price, etc. Consumers' reactions to the packaging of the new beverage and the advertising materials that are being used to promote the product may also be of interest. Along with these considerations, the experience of the café patron in terms of either drinking the beverage in the café or taking the drink 'to-go' may also be of relevance. In this situation the researcher will need to interview (individually and /or in focus groups) beverage drinkers about their experiences. Some form of projective test (these are covered later on in this book) may be employed to gain feedback on packaging and advertising options whilst observation may be made of actual consumer behaviour with the beverage within the café and on the streets outside.

With different types of research approaches several interviewers/research workers may be employed who have the responsibility for the project as a whole. These different research procedures, and the people conducting them, must be scheduled effectively to allow for the research project to run on time, to ensure that the data arising from one procedure informs later procedures, and perhaps most importantly, to provide a framework for bringing the different research procedures together so that the original research questions are addressed unambiguously. This latter point is of particular importance as each of the research procedures may produce different types of data (interviews = unstructured verbal accounts; observations = video footage that is then coded into pre-selected behaviour types; projective techniques = collages produced individually by beverage drinkers, etc.). This variety of pro-

---

5   Indeed, in the research project presented in the Appendices the authors suggest that students include all of the research approaches in this book.

cedures used in qualitative consumer research makes the direct comparison between results of these various procedures potentially problematic. Consequently, what is required is a clear framework for bringing the different results together to produce a comprehensible final report.

However, if you use a template that is too rigid or prescriptive upon the data under analysis you will restrict responses in the data and much of the rich individuality of the reactions may be lost. The mapping sentence has been found to be a tool that provides a framework for managing and planning a research project whilst being flexible enough not to impose a structure on responses.

In this course of study the mapping sentence will be used as a mechanism for structuring and formally planning/managing research projects. When used as a research design template, the mapping sentence is able to bring together many aspects of the research area and to display how these different research elements may be amalgamated. The project-management mapping sentence is able to coordinate disparate aspects of a research project to enable the researcher to appreciate and plan the project in a way that maximizes the usefulness of each of the parts of the project whilst allowing an appreciation of the combined components of the project as a whole.

Further Reading

Canter, D (ed.) (1985) *Facet Theory: Approaches to Social Research,* New York: Springer Verlag.

Dancer, L. S. (1990) Introduction to Facet Theory and its Applications. *Applied Psychology: An International Review, 39*(4), 365–377.

Guttman, R., and Greenbaum, C.W. (1998) Facet Theory: Its Development and Current Status, *European Psijchologist, 3*(1), pp. 13–36.

Hackett, P.M.W., and Foxall, G.R. (1997) Consumers' evaluations of an international airport: a facet theoretical approach, *The International Review of Retail, Distribution and Consumer Research, 7*(4), p. 339–349.

Hackett, P.M.W. (2014a) *Facet Theory and the Mapping Sentence: Evolving Philosophy, Use and Application,* Basingstoke; Palgrave.

Hackett, P.M.W (2014b) A Facet Theory Model for Integrating Contextual and Personal Experiences of International Students, *Journal of International Students, 4*(2), 163–176.

Hatori, T., Kawayoke, T., Kobayashi, K., Natsume, T., and Fujisaki, E. (2006) Protocol Analysis of a Public Debate Using Facet Theory, *Infrastructure Planning Review, 23*, pp. 91–102.

Hornik, J. (1976) A Circumplex Model for the Behavioral Constructs Towards Television Advertising, *Journal of the Academy of Marketing Science, 4*(1), pp. 484–503.

Hornik, J., Cohen, E.H., and Amar, R. (2007) A Facet Metatheoretical Approach to Advance Consumer Behaviour Knowledge, *Psychology and Marketing, 24*(9), pp. 787–813.

Hornik, J., Cohen, E., and Amar, R. (2009) Theory construction and data analysis in marketing communication: A facet analytical approach, *Journal of Marketing Communications, 15*(1), p. 35–54.

Landsheer, J., and Boeije, H. (2010) In search of content validity: facet analysis as a qualitative method to improve questionnaire design, *Quality & Quantity, 2010, 44*(1), pp. 59–69.

Lans, A. van der. (2006) *On the Structure of Measurements in Facet Theory Questionnaire Design and Data Analysis using Facet Approach Multidimensional Scaling with Regional Restrictions for Facet Theory: An Application to Levi's Political Protest Data,* Rotterdam: Erasmus Research Institute of Management (ERIM), Rotterdam School of Management and the Erasmus School of Economics (ESE) at Erasmus University Rotterdam.

Van Den Wittenboer, G. (2001) On the Structure of Measurements in Facet Theory, *Quality and Quantity, 35*(1), pp. 77–89.

Wu, J., Kim, A., and Koo, J. (2015) Co-design visual merchandising in 3D virtual stores: a facet theory approach, *International Journal Of Retail & Distribution Management, 43*(6), 538–560.

Chapter 3. Research Ethics

Conducting research with human subjects

Ethics is the area of study that involves investigation, organization and protection of societal concepts of right and wrong behaviour. There are multiple ways in which ethics relates to research.

The information that arises from human subjects in research studies may sometimes be harmful, damaging, or embarrassing for participants: embarrassment in particular is a very real possibility in classroom based research projects. This is in part due to the authority accorded to the experimenter and the fact that the information provided might be widely distributed and beyond the experimenter's control. A good example of this is the inappropriate revelation of participants' medical data. However, any type of information about an individual or group can be potentially damaging (especially in terms of their privacy) to respondents and others.

History of ethics in research

Modern research ethics began during the Nuremberg Trials for Nazi war criminals in 1946–1947. In the trials, also known as the Doctors' Trial, 23 Nazi doctors were prosecuted for allegedly conducting torturous and terrible experiments, as well as other less barbaric investigations, upon prisoners of concentration camps. The doctors carried out these procedures in the name of conducting research to test the extremes to which the human body could be pushed in order to establish the most rapid and efficient ways of killing people. The Nuremberg Code (Annas and Grodin, 1995) developed out of these trials and the subsequent prosecutions.

The Nuremberg Code states 10 basic ethical principles (these were all actions that the doctors violated). The 10 principles are:

1/ Participants in research must voluntarily consent to participating.
2/ The aims of the research project must benefit society.
3/ The research that is being undertaken must be based upon sound theory and must previously have employed animal testing.
4/ Any unnecessary physical and mental suffering must be avoided during the research.
5/ Research should not be permitted if the research project outcomes include potential serious injury or death.
6/ Participants' risks and benefits associated with undertaking the research must be commensurate.
7/ Participants must be protected from harm during the experiment.
8/ Those carrying out the experiments must be scientifically qualified.

9/ Human participants must have the right to withdraw/discontinue their participation whenever they wish.

10/ If there is any belief that continuing an experiment may result in harm or death to participants, those conducting an experiment must be ready to terminate the experiment.

Following the Nuremburg Code, the Declaration of Helsinki (Schmidt and Frewer, 2007) was the next major step forward in the development of ethical research practice. This Declaration was developed by the World Medical Association in 1964 and has been updated several times, most recently in 2008. The Declaration plays a mainstay role in human research ethics by placing moral obligations upon doctors and physicians within the context of their medical treatment and research activities.

The Declaration of Helsinki contains the basic components of the Nuremberg Code, yet includes additional consideration for the vulnerability of human subjects in clinical research. The Declaration of Helsinki states:

1/ That research projects must be reviewed and approved by an independent investigator

2/ That the supervision of the research is by a medically qualified person who takes responsibility for the research for subject welfare

3/ That research results must be accurate

4/ That informed consent is obtained within ethically recognized procedures from all participants

5/ That there are special rules for research with children and other vulnerable groups

6/ That experimental treatments on human subjects must be evaluated and monitored

7/ The importance of establishing an appropriate environment and procedure when undertaking medical research

In 1978 the Belmont Report was published by the US National Commission for the Protection of Human Subjects of Biomedical and Behavioral Research. The Belmont Report provides details about:

1/ The ethical principles for undertaking research with human subjects

2/ What constitutes medical practice and what constitutes research

3/ The need to respect persons within research and the need for beneficence and justice

4/ How the above principles must be applied within a framework of informed consent that embodies a respect for all participants, the assessment of risks to and benefits for all participants, and that subjects should be selected from the population that will benefit from the results/consequences of the research rather than being from an easily obtainable population who may not benefit from the research.

In many countries (including the United States) laws and regulations have been implemented to make research more responsible and to protect not only humans, but also animal subjects and the environment. However, the Nuremberg Code, the Declaration of Helsinki and the Belmont Report (United States National Commission for the Protection of Human Subjects of Biomedical and Behavioural Research, 1978) are all historically important in the development of ethical research practices and still have a profound effect upon the maintenance of research which is of universally acceptable quality and where laws are determined for transgressing ethical codes.

Development of Ethical Guides

Subsequent to the development of the above codes and declarations, there have been many regulatory documents developed for a wide variety of professional groups. These codes have been local, national, and international in their outlook but have tended to adopt the following set of core principles for research with human subjects:

1/ Human life and health is always more important than research
2/ Informed voluntary consent must be obtained from all subjects
3/ It must always be possible for a study to be discontinued at any time without any penalty to the study's participants
4/ The reasonable expectations of potential social benefits must be proportionate to the potential risks individual participants are asked to take
5/ Protective measures must be put in place for participants
6/ The findings that arise from human subject research must be beneficial to society
7/ No specific populations of individuals can receive either an excessive weight of research procedures or can be excluded from participation unless there is an extremely good reason for so doing
8/ Those who are responsible for conducting research must be appropriately trained and qualified researchers
9/ Research must be carefully designed to avoid any research procedures that may in any way injure research participants
10/ Research must be discontinued if a procedure may harm participants in any way

Institutional Review Boards (IRBs)

In many countries (including the United States and the United Kingdom) an institutional review board is typically located within organizations that take part in research (i.e., universities). The members of these boards attempt to ensure that any research with human subjects undertaken within their institutional authority upholds ethical standards by attempting to identify and eliminate any potentially harmful projects prior to their commencement[6]. In both the United States and United Kingdom, human subject research must be approved by an institutional review board prior to the research being conducted when: the research is funded by federal sources; an institute decides to participate voluntarily in the institutional review board review process even if it is not federally funded; the findings of the research are submitted for publication. In the Unites States the Food and Drug Administration may also be involved in reviewing the ethicality of a research proposal.

Institutional Review Boards review research proposals with a "globally" ethical outlook and attempt to identify issues that the researchers themselves may not have considered. An institutional review board will ensure that the lead applicant of a research project is professionally qualified and that all consent forms and other research related materials are easily understood by potential participants to facilitate the possibility of a truly comprehensive informed voluntary consent. The institutional review board also attempts to take a more detached perspective in balancing a wide range of potential risks and benefits to the participants that may arise from the research. The institutional review board may also offer appropriate compensation to research study participants.

Because institutional review boards often have to assess risks and benefits that may arise from research, they are not only constituted by appropriately qualified medical staff and other scientists, but also ethicists, research experts, and members of the general public. This mixed membership allows discussions to have a much wider range of applicability.

Informed consent

Researchers gathering informed consent from potential respondents means:

1/ Ensuring respondents are aware of the research they are volunteering for before they provide consent, this includes:
   – the aims and procedures of the research,
   – possible risks and expected benefits,

---

6   However, see Cohen and Lynch (2014) for a review of the possible negative consequences of institutional review boards.

- being able to ask questions,
- having the opportunity to withdraw at any time from the research.

2/ The investigator must ensure that consent is based upon comprehension and he or she must adapt information to be understandable to every participant irrespective of:
- intelligence levels,
- maturity,
- language ability.

3/ The participant must be free to consent to being a subject, or not, with no manipulation involved.

Privacy, anonymity, confidentiality and data management

Participant privacy is important and participants have the right to expect that their data will not be revealed beyond the extent to which they agreed when they signed the informed consent document. This means that the researcher must stipulate in the informed consent procedure the following details:

1/ The extent to which the data gathered from a participant will be publicly available and to what extent and in what ways the data will be confidential:
- personal and identifying information is to be gathered and kept **confidential** with access available to only certain specified people. If this is the case the extent of availability must be explained.

2/ Whether participants will be **anonymous**:
- no data will be gathered from which anyone (including the researchers) will be able to identify a participant.

3/ How the data will be retained (digital, hardcopy, etc.), where, and for how long.

4/ How the data will be eventually destroyed.

5/ Which persons other than the researcher(s) (if any) will have access to the data.

Thus far we have only considered human subjects. However, and whilst we will not present details in this book, more recently the Animal Welfare Act (in the United States) and other legislation in many countries, have set out a series of regulations and guidelines for conducting research with animals.

Data management issues include conducting research that is ethical and truthful. Data management is closely related to privacy issues and incorporates the truthful collection of data, what will happen to this data, and who will have access to this. Investigators must explicitly address these critical issues of the research process and produce an adequate data management plan.

The last of these issues under discussion, the sharing and publishing of results, may be a particular problem for researchers, as conducting scientific research requires official dissemination, and stress is often placed upon academic researchers to publish. However, investigators and their institutions are also wary of sharing what is in fact their intellectual property, yet sharing data and the results that arise from analysis of those results can add to the verification of the findings. A balance must be sought between sharing and protecting data. Some funding bodies require the submission of a plan for result dissemination prior to grants being awarded. The research team should retain data and other materials associated with a research project until a time when the data becomes obsolete and thus un-publishable. Consequently, prior to the start of a research project you must answer the following questions:

1/ Who will take charge and be responsible for the design of data collection procedures?
2/ Who is in charge of actual data collection?
3/ What procedures will be employed to gather the data?
4/ What type of data will be gathered (as previously mentioned, anonymous, confidential, or public)?
5/ What are the privacy issues associated with the project and how will these be addressed?
6/ Who is responsible for verifying the completeness and quality of data?
7/ Who is responsible for checking the accuracy of the interpretations of data?

Conflict of interest

An important area where qualitative researchers need to consider ethics is when there are issues concerning conflicts of interest. Such problems arise when an individual or organization has commitments and responsibilities outside of a research project, and these interests are in conflict with their obligations to a research project. When these conflicts exist, the researcher's work may be seen as biased and the results may be questioned. Examples of conflicts of interest include: when a researcher holds investments in a company related to the services or products being investigated, or a company is associated with the source of research funding. It is important for researchers to attempt to identify possible conflict of interests and find solutions to these before they compromise their projects.

The institutional review board looks for possible conflict of interests in proposals and will ask investigators to address them and may even suggest ways to combat the problem. Thus, researchers are often asked to declare financial conflicts of interest along with similar financial undertakings that their spouses or dependents may have.

Research Misconduct

Another area that must concern the qualitative researcher is that of research misconduct. Misconduct may either be consciously committed, may be comprised of reckless behaviours, or can consist of acts of omission (things that the researcher should have done but did not do). It is likely that most misconduct will be due to negligence, mistakes, or unintentional actions. These forms of misbehaviours are usually addressed and punished at the institutional level. Misconduct, if severe enough, may result in criminal prosecution although overwhelming evidence must support all allegations. For example, misconduct may involve falsifying or fabricating results (this may constitute a crime) or plagiarism.

Further reading

Allmark, P. (2002) The ethics of research with children. *Nurse Researcher, 10*(2):7–19.

Amdur, R.J., and Bankert, E.A. (2015*) Institutional Review Board Member Handbook,* Burlington, MA: Jones & Bartlett Learning.

Annas, G.J., and Grodin, M.A. (eds.) (1995) The Nazi Doctors and the Nuremberg Code: Human Rights in Human Experimentation, Oxford: Oxford University Press.

Cohen, I.G., and Lynch, H.F. (eds.) (2014) Human Subjects Research Regulation: Perspectives on the Future (Basic Bioethics), Cambridge, MA: The MIT Press.

Comstock, G. (2013) *Research Ethics: A Philosophical Guide to the Responsible Conduct of Research,* (Cambridge Medicine), Cambridge: Cambridge University Press.

Couzin, J. (2003) Human subjects. Crossing a frontier: research on the dead. *Science, 299*(5603): 29–30.

Garrett, J.R. (ed.) (2012) The Ethics of Animal Research: Exploring the Controversy (Basic Bioethics), Cambridge, MA: The MIT Press.

Gil, E.F, and. Bob, S. (1999) Culturally competent research: an ethical perspective. *Clinical Psychology Review, 19*(1): 45–55.

Heider, D., and Massanari, A.L. (eds.) (2012) *Digital Ethics: Research and Practice (Digital Formations),* Pieterlen, CH: Peter Lang Publishing Inc.

Hubrecht, R.C. (2014) The Welfare of Animals Used in Research: Practice and Ethics (UFAW Animal Welfare), New York: Wiley-Blackwell.

LeCompte, M.D. and Schensul, J.J. (2015) Ethics in Ethnography: A Mixed Methods Approach (Ethnographer's Toolkit, Second Edition), Lanham, MD: AltaMira.

Malacrida, C. (2007) Reflexive Journaling on Emotional Research Topics: Ethical Issues for Team Researchers, *Qualitative Health Research, 17*; 1329–1339. DOI: 10.1177/1049732307308948

Mertens, D.M., and Ginsberg, P.E. (2008) *The Handbook of Social Research Ethics,* Thousand Oaks, CA: Sage.

Miller, T., Birch, M., Mauthner, M, and Jessop, J. (eds.) (2012) *Ethics in Qualitative Research,* Thousand Oaks, CA: Sage.

National Bioethics Advisory Commission Report (1998) *Research Involving Persons with Mental Disorders that may Affect Decision-Making Capacity.* http://www.georgetown.edu/research/nrcbl/nbac/capacity/TOC.htm

National Bioethics Advisory Commission Report. (2001) *Ethical and Policy Issues in International Research: Clinical Trials in Developing Countries.* http://www.georgetown.edu/research/nrcbl/nbac/pubs.html

O'Leary, Z. (2013) *The Essential Guide to Doing Your Research Project,* Thousand Oaks, CA: Sage.

Pasquerella, L. (2002) Confining choices: should inmates' participation in research be limited? *Theoretical Medicine & Bioethics, 23*(6): 519–536.

Phoenix, J.A. (2002) Ethical considerations of research involving minorities, the poorly educated and/or low-income populations. *Neurotoxicology & Teratology, 24*(4): 475–476.

Rose, S.L., and Pietri, C.E. (2002) Workers as research subjects: a vulnerable population. *Journal of Occupational & Environmental Medicine, 44*(9): 801–805.

Schmidt, U., and Frewer, A. (2007) *History and Theory of Human Experimentation: The Declaration of Helsinki and Modern Medical Ethics (Geschichte Und Philosophie Der Medizin. History and Philosophy of Medicine),* Stuttgart: Franz Steiner Verlagby.

Shamoo, A.E., and Resnik, D.B. (2015) *Responsible Conduct of Research,* Oxford: Oxford University Press

Stark, L. (2012) *Behind Closed Doors: IRBs and the Making of Ethical Research (Morality and Society Series),* Chicago: University Of Chicago Press.

Stevens, P.E., and Pletsch, P.K. (2002) Informed consent and the history of inclusion of women in clinical research. *Health Care for Women International, 23*(8): 809–819.

United States National Commission for the Protection of Human Subjects of Biomedical and Behavioral Research, (1978) *The Belmont report: Ethical principles and guidelines for the protection of human subjects of research,* Ann Arbor, MI: University of Michigan Library

Section 2 – Approaches to Qualitative Research Methods in Consumer Psychological Research

Chapter 4. Projective Techniques

What are projective techniques?

To begin our consideration of the more common qualitative research strategies used in consumer behaviour investigations, we will look at projective techniques. This broad class of research procedures is used by investigators to delve deeply into a consumer's inner beliefs and attitudes by gathering data that may indicate more of the subconscious understandings of a product or service than the consumer's conscious rationalizations allow. With this intention investigators employ varied materials and designs in attempts to bypass these conscious filters surrounding human being's normally controlled behaviour. Projective techniques are used to project the contents of the sub-conscious directly into the creative responses of participants who are completing one of these procedures. Projective techniques are flexible and can be modified into a multitude of variants.

Projective techniques encountered within mainstream psychology usually refer to projective tests of personality. These tests require a person to respond to a stimulus that is ambiguous in nature. An example of this is the Rorschach Ink-Blot Test in which a person is presented with a series of equivocally shaped ink splotches and asked to describe of what the shape reminds them. The rational behind this procedure is that the response to the ambiguous stimuli reveals hidden emotions or thoughts, perhaps even inner conflicts, that the person being tested projects upon the inkblots.

In marketing and consumer research, projective techniques are used in attempts to discover and disclose consumers' subconscious beliefs, emotions, etc., about a product, service or concept. Investigators use projective techniques to ask respondents to project their feelings and thoughts about a target product, service, or concept onto something other than the target itself (for example, an ink-blot). Other approaches require the completion of sentences, describing who a brand or product would be if it were a person, and a wide variety of other imaginative methods. Another important component of a projective technique is that when respondents are asked to explain their answers, there is an assumption being made by the researchers that a respondent's explanations enable the researcher to understand subconscious processes. In addition to explanations, participants are often asked to provide further information and details associated with these responses.

Projective techniques are used widely and are fun for everyone concerned. A caveat is needed, however, as care must be employed due to the imprecision of the stimulus material and the highly subjective nature of responses. Replies often need considerable interpretation in order for the investigator to make sense of a consumer's reference to a product, service or concept. An example of a technique would be a creativity session in which a participant is asked to draw or create a collage from physical objects or digital images that represent a particular product to the consumer.

Another example could be filling in empty speech balloons on a sketch of stick figures. For instance, two or three figures are drawn with three empty speech bubbles above one of the figures. One bubble is labelled 'I Think...,' another 'I Feel...,' and the other bubble is labelled 'I Am...'. The participant is then told that he is the stick figure with the balloons and that the other stick figures represent friends, partners, etc. The stick figures are then located in a storyline. For example, the investigator explains that the figures represent the participant and his partner and their daughter. They have just entered a shopping mall and it is the week before Christmas. The participant is then asked to finish the three sentences in the context of the storyline to indicate what he or she would be thinking and feeling (I think..., I feel...., I am....).

A different format of projective technique can be found in mapping techniques. These approaches, as their name suggests, requires participants to complete a map-making task. The precise task can be varied but two common examples are the semantic mapping and mind mapping procedures. In semantic mapping the participant locates a number of items in semantic (personally meaningful) space. This semantic space is defined by drawing a cross on a large card, paper, or board, etc. The two intersecting lines form axes that constitute personally meaningful space. The crossed lines may be supplied by the researcher or solicited from the participant. Items are then arranged in the space created by the axes. As with the axes, the items may either be supplied by the researcher or solicited from participants. In supplying the axes the researcher is able to guide participants' responses and to produce findings that are comparable between respondents. In soliciting the axes the researcher allows the maximum degree of freedom of responses a participant may provide. However, these supplied axes may not directly relate to the question the researcher is investigating.

An illustration may aid your comprehension. Let us imagine the topic of interest is a recently developed automobile produced by a major manufacturer of motor vehicles. The production company may be interested to know how customers perceive their car in relation to new cars from competing automobile makers. In this situation a researcher may define a semantic space by drawing a cross with a vertical axis and writing the words 'poor quality' at its base and 'high quality' at the top. The researcher also supplies labels for the horizontal axis by writing 'inexpensive' at the left end of the line and 'expensive' at the right end. Participants are then supplied with the names of 5–10 automobiles that the manufacturer believes are in direct competition with their new model. The participant is asked to write the name of each of the car models on the semantic space so that cars seen as: poor quality and inexpensive = bottom left; poor quality and expensive = bottom right; high quality and inexpensive = top left; high and expensive = top right.

Instead of providing the axes names or the items to be positioned, the researcher may ask respondents to supply the axes that have a meaning for them in relation to the research topic and /or to supply the items for positioning. The researcher assigns axes and/or items when she or he has a clear idea of the consumer's understanding of a topic area. In the above example, researchers might believe that cost and quality are the important dimensions that differentiate the new car from its competitors (this belief might reflect the automobile manufacturer's research questions). The items (competing cars in the market) may also be elicited from participants if the manufacturer is uncertain of the competition. In order to provide as much useful information as possible about respondents' thoughts and activities whilst completing this procedure, the entire process is video recorded.

Mind mapping procedures are conducted using a similar support, such as a card, board, paper, etc., upon which participants are asked to write or draw (or upon which the moderator makes marks as instructed by the participant). In this procedure the name of a product, service or concept central to the research question is written in the middle of the board. Participants are then asked what comes to mind when they think about this word and their response is written down adjacent to it and then the two words are linked with a drawn line. This procedure is repeated three or four times until the original word has three to five other concepts radiating from it. The questioning and drawing/writing procedure is repeated with the radiating concepts. This process is repeated until the participant has produced a radiating web of concepts. Finally, respondents may be asked if any of the radiating concepts link with each other. Lines are drawn between the linked concepts. Participants are then asked to explain the connections they have drawn and these descriptions are written down on the support next to the lines.

An example using the same product as above, a new model of car, will serve as an illustration. The name of the car is written centrally and a participant is asked what comes to mind when she or he sees this name. She replies 'new' and the procedure is repeated. The words 'expensive', 'safe' and 'family' are elicited. The researcher then asks the participant what 'new' means to the participant when she thinks of cars? She responds 'untested,' 'advanced technology', and 'envy'. When the participant is asked to explain what 'expensive' means in relation to cars, she may say 'credit rating,' 'holiday in Peru', and 'parent.' This procedure is repeated for all of the radiating terms and then for the additional set of radiating concepts and the meanings behind each word or phrase are explored further. The words or phrases supplied by the participant will all have personal meanings, which must be analysed within the procedure. For example, when the words 'credit rating,' 'holiday in Peru' and 'parent' were provided by the participant, their meanings were unclear. By asking what the participant means by 'holiday in Peru' within the context of the new car, she might explain that if she buys the new car the planned holiday in Peru will have to be postponed: the purchasing decision will ultimately be a straight choice between the car and the holiday. On the other hand, the participant may tell the researcher that she said 'parent' because her father drove an earlier version of this model automobile. She has always associated this brand and model with the highest quality and this purchase is something to which she has always aspired. She sees the acquisition of this particular model as having arrived at the same grown-up level of automobile ownership as her father. Such comments have relevance in the positioning of the new model in the market place. As with all projective techniques the entire procedure is video recorded.

What questions do projective techniques answer?

All projective techniques attempt to answer a similar question in slightly different ways and with specific emphases. The overarching question that projectives address is: what are the unconscious or subconscious motives that a person has for behaving in the manner that he or she does? For example, it often appears that when a researcher asks consumers why they have purchased a certain item, the response given is usually a post-purchase rationalization for the consumer's behaviour. Indeed, this behaviour may be habitual and almost automatic and the consumer may not even be consciously aware of the choice processes undertaken when making their purchase decision. Whatever the reason for this lack of recognition or active suppression, projective techniques attempt to tap into the motives that a consumer has below the level of rationality and/or conscious awareness.

What are the limitations to projective techniques?

Practical limitations to projective techniques

If available, software can be used to create, manipulate, and edit mind maps, mood boards, collages, etc. However, this software may not often be available in class settings. This is not a great disadvantage as projective procedures are easily completed without software.

Cost limitations to projective techniques

Projective techniques have few cost implications and are often undertaken with a minimum of materials.

Bias limitations of projective techniques

The results or output of most projective techniques require the moderator to interpret these findings and such interpretations always contain bias.

Now You

Now, think about how you could incorporate one or several of these projective techniques into investigating your sample product or service. Which of the procedures seems interesting to you and why? How would you run the procedure, what hidden emotions and thoughts are you looking for in your participants?

Further reading

Bradley. N. (21013) *Marketing Research: Tools and Techniques,* Oxford: Oxford University Press.

Buzan, T., and Griffiths, C. (2014) *Mind Maps for Business: Using the Ultimate Thinking Tool to Revolutionise How You Work,* Harlow: Pearson Educational Ltd.

Cherrier, H. (2012) Using Projective Techniques to Consider the Societal Dimension of Healthy Practices: An Exploratory Study. *Health Marketing Quarterly, 29*(1), p. 82–95.

Ezan, P., Gollety, M., and Hémar-Nicolas, V. (2015) Drawing as Children's Language: Contributions of Psychology to the Enrichment of Research Methodologies Applied to Child Consumers, *Recherche et Applications en Marketing (English Edition), 30*(2), pp. 78–96.

Gámbaro, A., Parente, E., Roascio, A., and Boinbaser, L. (2014) Word Association Technique Applied to Cosmetic Products – A Case Study. *Journal Of Sensory Studies, 29*(2). 103–109.

Iacobucci, D. and Churchill, G.A. (2015)*Marketing Research: Methodological Foundations*, CreateSpace Independent Publishing Platform.

Kujala, S., Walsh, T., Nurkka, P., and Crisan, M. (2014) Sentence Completion for Understanding Users and Evaluating User Experience, *Interacting with Computers, 26*(3), pp. 238–255.

Leibowitz, M. (2014) *Interpreting Projective Drawings: A Self-Psychological Approach,* London: Routledge.

Mason, H. (1950) Projective Techniques in Marketing Research, *Journal of Marketing, 14*(5), pp. 649–656.

Morrison, M.A., Haley, E.E., Sheehan, K and Taylor, R.E. (2011) *Using Qualitative Research in Advertising: Strategies, Techniques, and Applications,* Thousand Oaks, CA: Sage Publications, Inc.

Murstein, B.I. (ed.) (1965) *Handbook of Projective Techniques,* Jackson, TN: Basic Books.Pich, C., and Dean, D. (2015) Qualitative Projective Techniques in Political Brand Image Research from the Perspective of Young Adults, *Qualitative Market Research: An International Journal, 18*(1). 115–144.

Soley, L.C., and Smith, A.L. (2008) *Projective Techniques For Social Science And Business Research,* Shirley, NY: The Southshore Press.

Vidal, L., Ares, G., and Giménez, A. (2013) Projective Techniques to Uncover Consumer Perception: Application of Three Methodologies to Ready-to Eat Salads, *Food Quality and Preference, 28*(1), pp.1–7.

Wassler, P., & Hung, K. (2014). Brand-as-Person versus Brand-as-User: An Anthropomorphic Issue in Tourism-related Self-Congruity Studies. *Asia Pacific Journal of Tourism Research, 20*(8), 839–859.

Chapter 5. Focus Groups

What are focus groups?

Focus groups, or focus group interviews (FGIs) as they are sometimes called, take the format of a group discussion. A moderator acts as a facilitator for the interactions in what are essentially contrived research debates. Thematic areas are identified and the facilitator guides the conversation around chosen topics. A good moderator says little but puts participants at ease, making sure that no individual dominates the group session and that all participants have their opinions heard.

Focus groups are well known and widely used within marketing research, consumer research, social research, and other investigative areas; however, they are not without their critics who state that focus groups produce clichéd answers, responses to please moderators, and other misinforming results. The optimal size of a focus group interview is dependent upon the project but is probably between 5 and 15 individuals and most commonly between 8 and 12.

Focus groups are good settings for idea generation and brainstorming, hence their popularity in marketing, product development, political marketing, etc. Focus group interviews are also excellent venues for disclosing the ways in which consumers use language to discuss products. Likes and dislikes may emerge and motives for product usage and purchases are often revealed. Researchers gain insights into consumer attitudes and perceptions in the form of prejudices, beliefs, needs, and emotional attachments. A good moderator is essential to manage group dynamics and to expose hidden knowledge that may often be unknown to the participants themselves.

Online focus groups

A more recent trend in focus groups is to conduct these interview procedures online. See, Liampuyyong, (2011) and also Hennick, (2014) for further details.

Advantages of using online focus groups:

1/ They are good ways to generate new ideas and participants may feel less inhibited to brainstorm online than in a face-to-face situation
2/ They are relatively low in cost
3/ They may be performed relatively quickly

4/ They are not bound by geography – respondents may be recruited to fit the needs of the research without the respondents having to attend a physical location

5/ They are good for generating ideas for further research

Disadvantages of online focus groups include:

1/ A lack of control over who is participating and any other influences that are effecting the online participant while she or he is taking part in the group discussion

2/ The moderator cannot keep participants on track as easily or motivate their interest

3/ Lack of moderator control means they may not be able to use all of their skills to the utmost

4/ It may be more difficult and less effective to use hands on procedures, such as sort procedures and other projective techniques in an online group

5/ Interpretation of what happens in the group may be more problematic and even more subjective

6/ The moderator may be unaware of or miss non-verbal components of participants' reactions

What questions do focus groups answer?

The main types of information that focus groups are able to provide are brainstorming or new idea generation. Focus groups are good sources for innovative solutions.

What are the limitations of focus groups?

The limitations of the focus group are those inherent in most group activities, for example: some individuals when in a group setting may be more concerned with their position in the group than the product in question; become a group opinion leader whilst others may follow; move to a more risky or a more conservative position than they would in an individual setting; etc.

Practical limitations to focus groups

Focus groups need to be located in relatively quiet settings where up to twenty people may be comfortably seated. Within the class setting either a classroom or the focus group room are suitable locations.

Focus groups can take up to two hours and this may be very difficult for students to manage. However, we suggest that focus groups performed for training purposes, i.e. as part of a research class, be limited to 20 minutes although this short duration does curtail the amount and depth of possible discussion. Yet, for students who have not previously conducted this type of session, 20 minutes is a good length to learn about the focus group as an active process and 20 minutes will yield a useful body of narrative.

Other practical limitations

1/ Respondents may feel shy/reluctant to discuss some issues in a group environment
2/ Not a good environment to delve in-depth into motives, reasons, etc., as this requires a one-to-one interviewer to respondent setting
3/ A poor moderator may have a large impact on the success of the focus group

Cost limitations of focus groups

Focus groups may be a relatively expensive research approach to conduct successfully. This is due to the requirements of the procedure for: a trained moderator; a specialized facility; recompense for participants; the cost of having the qualitative data analysed; etc.

Bias limitations of focus groups

Focus groups are potentially biased in the way that all group procedures are biased: responses given in a group setting may not be the individuals' opinion but rather an artefact of being in the group.

Now You

Given what you have learned about focus groups in this section, do you think this method may be suitable for your sample research project? How would you, as a facilitator, ensure that all group members can contribute to the discussion, what difficulties do you see in facilitating a focus group discussion?

Further reading

Bos, C., van der Lans, I.A., van Rijnsoever, F.J., van Trijp, H.C.M. (2013) Understanding consumer acceptance of intervention strategies for healthy food choices: a qualitative study, *BMC public health, 13*(1), 1073.

Bristol, T. and Fern, E.F. (2003) The effects of interaction on consumers' attitudes in focus groups, *Psychology and Marketing, 20*(5), pp. 433–454.

Bystedt, J., Lynn, S., and Potts, D. (2010) *Moderating to the Max: A Full-tilt Guide to Creative, Insightful Focus Groups and Depth Interviews,* Ithaca, NY: Paramount Market Publishing, Inc.

Carey, M.A., and Asbury, J-E. (2012) *Focus Group Research,* (Qualitative Essentials) Walnut Creek, CA: Left Coast Press.

Delbecq, A. L., van de Ven, A.H., and Gustafson, D.H. (1975) *Group Techniques for Program Planning,* Glenview, Ill: Scott, Foresman and Company.

Gavaravarapu, S.R.M., Vemula, S.R., Rao, P. Mendu, V.V.R., and Polasa, K. (2009) Focus Group Studies on Food Safety Knowledge, Perceptions, and Practices of School-Going Adolescent Girls in South India, *Journal of Nutrition Education and Behaviour, 41*(5), p. 340–346.

Greenbaum, T.L. (1999) *Moderating Focus Groups: A Practical Guide for Group Facilitation,* Thousand Oaks, CA: Sage Publications, Inc.

Hennick, M.M. (2014) *Focus Group Discussions,* (Understanding Qualitative Research) Oxford: Oxford University Press.

Kamberelis, G., and Dimitriadis, G. (2013) *Focus Groups: From structured interviews to collective conversations,* London: Routledge.

Kleijnen, M., Lee, N., and Wetzels, M. (2009) An exploration of consumer resistance to innovation and its antecedents, *Journal of Economic Psychology, 30*(3), pp. 344–357.

Krueger, R.A., and Casey, M.A. (2014) *Focus Groups: A Practical Guide for Applied Research,* Thousand Oaks, CA: Sage Publications, Inc.

Liampuyyong, P. (2011) *Focus Group Methodology: Principle and Practice,* Thousand Oaks, CA: Sage Publications, Inc.

Meenaghan, T., and O' Sullivan, P. (2001) Sponsorship and advertising: A comparison of consumer perceptions, *Psychology and Marketing,18*(2), pp. 191–215.

Morgan, D. (1996a) *Focus Groups as Qualitative Research, Second Edition, (Qualitative Research Methods Series 16)* Thousand Oaks, CA: Sage Publications, Inc.

Morgan, D. L. (1996b) Focus Groups, *Annual Review of Sociology, 22,* 129–152.

Nelson, G., Lord, J., Ochocka, J., Mccubbin, M., and Bostock, J. (2001) Empowerment and mental health in community: narratives of psychiatric consumer/ survivors, *Journal of Community & Applied Social Psychology, 11*(2), pp. 125–142.

Phillips, D.M., and Hallman, W.K. (2013) Consumer Risk Perceptions and Marketing Strategy: The Case of Genetically Modified Food, *Psychology & Marketing, 30*(9), Page 739–748.

Niu, H-jJ., Chiang, Y-S., and Tsai, H-t. (2012) An Exploratory Study of the Otaku Adolescent Consumer, *Psychology & Marketing, 29*(10), pp. 712–725.

Stewart, D.W. and Shamdasani, P.N. (2014) *Focus Groups: Theory and Practice, (*Applied Social Research Methods) Thousand Oaks, CA: Sage Publications, Inc.

Stöttinger, B., and Penz, E. (2015) Concurrent Ownership of Brands and Counterfeits: Conceptualization and Temporal Transformation from a Consumer Perspective, *Psychology & Marketing, 32*(4), pp. 373–391.

Vega-Zamora, M., Torres-Ruiz, F.J., Murgado-Armenteros, E.M., and Parras-Rosa, M. (2014) Organic as a Heuristic Cue: What Spanish Consumers Mean by Organic Foods, *Psychology & Marketing, 31*(5), p. 349–359.

Chapter 6. In-Depth Interviews

What are in-depth interviews?

In-depth interviews, or as they are sometimes called, depth interviews, are one-to-one interviews between an interviewer and an interviewee. This form of interview will typically be unstructured (an interview without any of the questions decided upon by the interviewer before the meeting – the interviewee guides the discussion as she or he wishes) or at most semi-structured (an interview in which the interviewer asks a few main questions and the interviewee has free rein to answer and expand upon these questions). It is unlikely that the interview will be a structured interview, i.e., an interview conducted from a set of questions that the interviewer asks and the interviewee answers. Rather, the investigator will tend to conduct the interview from a series of broad questions that have been selected to cover the important aspects associated with the research subject matter. Each of these topic areas may have a number of probe questions. In this course we will employ a semi-structured approach. When conducted in the commercial sector the interview will usually last for one to two hours. However, in a class, the procedure may be shorter. The overall idea of the in-depth interview is for the interviewer to explore with the participant the area or sub-areas of the research.

Thus, the aim of the in-depth interview is to use the one-to-one, face-to face setting to allow the interviewer to probe into the respondents' beliefs, attitudes and opinions in order to facilitate greater meaning and understanding. The interviewer will use an approach that employs less direct, 'counselling' types of questions and probes. These take extra time when compared to more direct/structured interviewing procedures, which allow, and indeed encourage, the interviewee to say as much about the research area as is useful. When you are conducting an in-depth interview, you should attempt to say as little as you can. The research results will not benefit from hearing the interviewer's opinions. Better research occurs if the interviewer restricts himor herself to introducing broad topics and only speaking when participants' responses are ambiguous. By using interjections such as: "It is interesting to hear you say that, can you tell me more?" or "Uhm, can you explain what you mean by that?" the investigator encourages clarification, but withholds his or her opinion.

What questions do in-depth interviews answer?

Interviewees are often recruited to represent individuals who are well informed about the product or are super-users of the product or service. A carefully selected group of participants offers the skilled interviewer the opportunity to delve deeply into the participant's understanding. The questions answered are thus deeply personal and offer much potential insight into product and service attitudes, beliefs, and how these services and products are used.

What are the limitations to in-depth interviews?

Practical limitations to in-depth interviews

There are few practical limitations specifically associated with in-depth interviews but the procedure must be held somewhere that is quiet, where the interviewer and interviewee are uninterrupted, and where the interviewee feels at ease. As there is little technical equipment required (except for recording equipment), the in-depth interview may be held in many locations including the participant's home or in neutral public settings.

Cost limitations to in-depth interviews

A small amount of pertinent data may be produced from an in-depth interview when compared with other methods and this may not be cost or time efficient. Therefore, in-depth interviews should be conducted sparingly with carefully chosen respondents who have a depth of relevant knowledge and experience.

Bias limitations to in-depth interviews

In-depth interviews reflect a single participant's opinion or account and therefore do not answer questions about what other people or social groups may think, feel, or do. Furthermore, as the information that an interviewee provides is subjective and the questions that are asked are usually different for each person interviewed, the data that arises from an in-depth interview is not strictly comparable with responses from another in-depth interview.

Now You

When considering an IDI in order to explore consumers' beliefs and feelings about your chosen product or service, whom would you choose as the ideal partner for your interview? What would you ask him or her, how can you formulate your questions to make sure not to bias the respondent's answers?

Further reading

Atkinson, R.G. (1998) *The Life Story Interview, (Qualitative Research Methods)* Thousand Oaks, CA: Sage Publications, Inc.

Brinkmann, S., and Kvale, S. (2014) *InterViews: Learning the Craft of Qualitative Research Interviewing,* Thousand Oaks, CA: Sage Publications, Inc.

Corbin, J., & Morse, J. M. (2003) The Unstructured Interactive Interview: Issues of Reciprocity and Risks when Dealing with Sensitive Topics, *Qualitative Inquiry, 9,* 335–354.

Fontana, A., and Frey, J. (2000) The Interview from Structured Questions to Negotiated Text, in Denzin, N.K., and Lincoln, Y.S. (eds.) *Handbook of Qualitative Research,* Thousand Oaks (California): Sage. pp. 361–376.

Holstein, J. A., and Gubrium, J. F. (1997) The active interview, in D. Silverman (ed.), *Qualitative research: Theory, method, and practice* (pp. 113–130). London: Sage.

Josselson, R. (2013) Interviewing for Qualitative Inquiry: A Relational Approach, New York: The Guilford Press

Mason, J. (2002) Qualitative Researching, London. Sage.

Morris, A. (2015) A Practical Introduction to In-depth Interviewing, Thousand Oaks, CA: Sage Publications, Inc.

Rubin, H.J., Rubin, I.S. (2011) Qualitative Interviewing: The Art of Hearing Data, Thousand Oaks, CA: Sage Publications, Inc.

Seidman, I. (2012) Interviewing as Qualitative Research: A Guide for Researchers in Education and the Social Sciences, New York: Teachers College Press.

Chapter 7. Ethnography

What is ethnography?

The etymological source of the word ethnography is Ancient Greek and the original meaning is useful to understanding its current usage. Ethnos (ἔθνος) means people, nation, or folk, whilst graphia (γράφω) means to write, record, or represent, and thus combined, the term refers to describing or reporting the ways human beings live. Ethnography has developed out of the field of anthropology, which uses empirical information to produce understandings of all aspects of the human species: its origins, evolution, commonalities and differences. Ethnography now is used by a variety of social sciences to investigate the lived reality of individuals or groups within cultures. Ethnography means that the researcher, or ethnographer, participates in the everyday lives of subjects and thereby systematically assesses questions about their culture. More recently ethnography has become a tool for marketing and communication studies.

Ethnographic approaches to consumer research (and to other forms of social research) may be defined in two ways. First, ethnography is a process in qualitative culturally located research. Secondly, ethnography has the explicit intention of providing an interpretation and understanding of culturally relevant behaviours and meanings. Ethnographers do not simply report events; they attempt to explain what they encounter and are concerned with holistic research that strives to produce credible realities. These realities may include many forms of background detail gathered through watching, listening, and asking questions to allow greater understanding of the social lives of the group of people who are of interest. Coleman and Simpson (undated) defined ethnography as:

> "...the recording and analysis of a culture or society, usually based on participant-observation and resulting in a written account of a people, place or institution."

Ethnographies take the form of case studies that are produced in order to provide insight into unfamiliar and often commonplace activities of everyday life. Within a consumer and marketing setting these studies are sometimes able to provide revelatory understandings of what a product, service, or concept means to a cultural group and the ways in which these are purchased, used, and modified. Ethnographies are particularly useful for revealing suggestions for product and service innovation. In consumer research settings, ethnography is typified by its use of several qualitative research approaches and data types. Data analysis also follows a typical structure; that of the identification and coding of themes and key issues. Exceptions and contradictions to usual patterns are also identified.

Example 1: The opportunities of bringing a British compact car to the US

Ethnographical Study:

To investigate the specific wants of US customers for a British compact car, which has a strong brand image of youthful fun. This will be undertaken by researchers visiting potential purchasers and acknowledged 'early adopters' in customers' own homes.

Questions:
1/ When and in what settings is there a demand for a trendy compact car?
2/ Who is the usual driver of existing compact cars in the family?
3/ Who else uses the compact and when?
4/ What determines the choice of operating a compact car?
5/ From these observations and insights – is it possible to come to any conclusions about consumer segments as these relate to compact cars, such as: gender, age, socio-economic class, etc.?
6/ What, if any, conclusions can be made about compact cars and different cultures?

In this example, by conducting research in the homes (or other daily-life settings related to car usage) the consumer ethnographer is able to provide the car company with powerful understandings about real product requirements. For example, an ethnographical study of this type may reveal stylish foreign compact cars tend to be driven by younger family members but also by parents who were often observed to take beverages with them in the car and to enter into a youthful spirit when driving. These findings may suggest a new line of advertising to attract older users.

To summarise: within a consumer setting ethnography may assist a company to understand:

1/ Existing and/or potential customers in terms of cultural fashions, tendencies, and lifestyles
2/ How social and cultural factors influence consumers' use of a commodity or service; how customers discover goods, their selection process and subsequent explorations; their decision-making practices, etc., in regard to a product and service
3/ How a company's services or goods fit into the daily lives of customers

Ethnographies are conducted in the real-life setting of a product or service's usage, such as the consumer's homes, offices, sporting or entertainment facility, etc. These types of environments are chosen as they enable researchers to observe naturally occurring product related behaviours and to ask follow-up questions. Wherever they are conducted, observation sessions may last for several hours. Ethnographic research offers the investigator greater comprehension of customer trends, problems, likes, etc., by not only addressing the ways in which consumers use products/services, but also how they adapt product and service usage to meet their own needs. Ethnographic inquiries may thus lead to greater understanding or even novel realisations from which products or services may be improved.

Ethnography can take a variety of forms but in essence will contain some degree of participant observation (see DeWalt and DeWalt, 2010; and Jorgensen, 1989). Sometimes the word ethnography is used interchangeably with the term qualitative research to denote any investigative approach that is attempting to yield complex and in-depth-understandings of real-life social or cultural activities. We wish however to draw a distinction between more traditional ethnography and that which has become a pseudonym for qualitative research. These two distinct forms of research are sometimes identified as 'the big-E and little-e ethnography' (See Carole Schmidt address this division in chapter 9 in Hackett, 2015).

Big-E ethnography is typically conceived as a participant observation procedure and is usually undertaken over an expanse of months or indeed years. This lengthy period of being in the field usually requires researchers to become full members of the culture they are investigating. Big-E ethnography is the currency of anthropologists and sociologists based within university departments. However, when ethnography is undertaken within a commercial setting such protracted research studies are usually impracticable. This is where little-e ethnography comes in. This form of research is undertaken over a much shorter time period than Big-E ethnography. Researchers do not spend months in a community but employ participant observation as their technique over a period of hours, days, or weeks, and thus are unlikely to become a fully immersed member of the culture studied. Since time is a costly commodity and products or services are competing in a fierce market, taking months to view cultural usage is inappropriate. As well as shorter-term participant observation, little-e ethnography may also be defined as, *the use of many different qualitative research procedures with the aim of revealing the cultural significance of these products or services to their users or potential users.* The types of procedures are illustrated in the 10 qualitative approaches to research that are explored in this book.

It is important to take notice that in this course of study, ethnography is taken to mean short-term participant observation.

What questions does ethnography answer?

How are our products and services used and experienced within an everyday setting by the actual people who use them? Further questions that apply to the cultural significance of our topic may also be investigated. Furthermore, research may be undertaken into cultural adaptations of products and services in a real world environment. In these circumstances, it is possible for the researcher to view consumers from the investigated cultures in order to reveal ways the consumers have adopted and/or adapted a product or service to their own needs.

What are the limitations to ethnography?

Practical limitations to ethnography

The difficulties associated with the ethnographic procedures explored in this text will involve the challenges associated with the effects of a researcher's presence upon the behaviour of the studied individuals. These predicaments have been previously mentioned but include participants changing their behaviours to appear in a certain way to the researcher.

Cost limitations to ethnography

Ethnographic procedures are expensive because they are labour intensive. To employ a skilled researcher and to place him or her within a culturally located situation over an extended time period is costly.

Analysing the potentially large amount of qualitative data that may arise from an ethnographic study can also be time consuming, and therefore, expensive as well.

Bias limitations

As with most qualitative research methods there is potential for bias arising during the interpretation of the output from an ethnographic procedure.

The possibilities for the introduction of bias during the field-study period are considerable. This bias is often related to the influence of the researcher's presence upon the behaviour of the participants, as well as the negotiated interactive situations that develop between researcher and participants. The notion of the thin line exemplifies the distance between a researcher who is accepted within a culture but is still in the position to gather unbiased data and a researcher who becomes too emotionally involved in the culture and finds him- or herself identifying with the studied group. This process of "going native" may easily happen due to the intense interactions that both the researcher and participant experience.

Now You

If you wanted to use a (little-e) ethnographic approach as part of your sample research project, which would be the ideal "culture", i.e. group of persons, to explore? How would you gain access to this group, how can you make sure you maintain an objective distance while still gathering experiential data about how people interact with, think about, and like the product or service you are investigating?

Further reading

Coleman, S., and Simpson, B. Ethnography, (undated) *Glossary of terms, Discover Anthropology London: Royal Anthropological Institute,* http://www.discover anthropology.org.uk/about-anthropology/glossaryofterms.html.

Davies, C.A. (2007) *Reflexive Ethnography: A Guide to Researching Selves and Others,* (The ASA Research Methods) London: Routledge.

DeWalt., K.M., and DeWalt, B.R. (2010) *Participant Observation: A Guide for Fieldworkers,* Lanham, MD: AltaMira Press.

Emerson, R.M., Fretz, R.I., and Shaw, L.L. (2011) Writing *Ethnographic Fieldnotes,* Second Edition (Chicago Guides to Writing, Editing, and Publishing) Chicago: University Of Chicago Press.

Fetterman, D.M. (2009) *Ethnography: Step-by-Step,* (Applied Social Research Methods) Thousand Oaks, CA: Sage Publications, Inc.

Jorgensen, D.L. (1989) *Participant Observation: A Methodology for Human Studies* (Applied Social Research Methods), Thousand Oaks, CA: Sage Publications, Inc.

Ladner, S. (2014) *Practical Ethnography: A Guide to Doing Ethnography in the Private Sector,* Walnut Creek, CA: Left Coast Press.

Maanen, J.V. (2001) *Tales of the Field: On Writing Ethnography,* Second Edition (Chicago Guides to Writing, Editing, and Publishing) Chicago: University Of Chicago Press.

Mariampolski, H. (2001) *Qualitative Market Research: A Comprehensive Guide,* Thousand Oaks, CA: Sage Publications, Inc.

Mariampolski, H. (2005) *Ethnography for Marketers: A Guide to Consumer Immersion,* Thousand Oaks, CA: Sage Publications, Inc.

Miller, J M. (2006) Covert Participant Observation: Reconsidering the Least Used Method, in Miller, J.M., and Tewksbury, R. (eds.) *Research Methods: A Qualitative Reader,* pp. 12–19. Upper Saddle River, NJ: Prentice Hall.

Schmidt, C. (2015) In-Depth Interviews, in, Hackett, P.M.W. (ed.) *Qualitative Methods in Consumer Psychology: Ethnography and Culture,* New York: Routledge.

Sunderland, P., and Denny, R.M. (2009) *Doing Anthropology in Consumer Research,* Walnut Creek, CA: Left Coast Press.

Wolcott, H.F. (2008) *Ethnography: A Way of Seeing, Lanham, MD:* AltaMira Press.

Chapter 8. Netnography

What is netnography?

Netnography is a relatively new qualitative consumer research procedure and is also known as digital, or online ethnography, terms, which indicate the source for this type of investigative practice. Netnography is different from the collection of archival or other online information about a product or service. Online ethnography, or netnography, comprises of the observation of groups of individuals associated with a product or a service in their natural behaviour location. This location is where consumers assemble online and ask each other questions or search for support and answers to product related enquiries. The sites where consumers meet may be hosted by the company that produces the product or service, by individual consumers with an interest in these goods, or it may be a sort of independent website that provides discussions and product reviews. In a commercial consumer setting netnographies require the investigator to become immersed in the online community through Internet forums, discussion groups, feedback comments, and dedicated websites that surround products and services. Such immersion may provide the opportunity for researchers to ask direct product related questions but more likely the netnographic process is one in which the investigator comes to understand consumers by spending time amongst them on the internet. In some cases, immersion may simply involve becoming a fly-on-the-wall within online discussion groups while garnering information about a product or service from the comments and interactions posted by the participants. It should be noted however that the variation between online and offline consumer behaviour is becoming less distinct as consumers spend more of their lives online.

Netnography is a comparatively recent but ever evolving research technique. Similarly ethical issues associated with the use of data from web forums or comments taken from customer feedback at sites such as Ecommerce are developing in complexity. However, to ensure practical and ethical rigor within a taught course setting, students may concentrate exclusively upon online data from customer discussions that are freely available and do not require attribution to any specific person.

Netnography research progresses through a series of stages during which the researcher needs to decide exactly what questions he is trying to answer and which sites s/he needs to observe. It is the task of the netnographer to collect online materials that provide information about the product of interest. This may take the form of online photographs, video and audio clips, user comments, blog postings, social media, etc., with the aim of investigating consumers' online-lives. As well as gathering these forms of data, other qualitative techniques are employed, such as participant observation and the posting of questions.

During data analysis, findings are arranged to demonstrate the meaning of the online conversations and to identify the role of social media. Key themes are determined and investigated using social media analytic tools (such as Socialmention.com) and thematic analysis programs (such as NUDIST, etc.). Images and texts gathered by the researcher are also organized under these themes.

What questions does netnography answer?

As more and more of our daily lives move online, so do the discussions that we have with other users of products and services. Netnography seeks to answer questions about how products or services are used and experienced. With any given consumer product, netnography attempts to understand and reveal consumers attitudes and behaviours associated with that product by allowing the researcher to become thoroughly immersed within the online community that surrounds a product or service[7].

Netnography is able to answer questions such as:

1/ In which areas are online consumer groups engaging?
2/ What are the topics they are discussing?
3/ By using this knowledge, how can a company better understand why their customers behave as they do (i.e., purchase, do not purchase)?

As a consequence of the answers to these questions, a company may be able to ask:

1/ How may a company better align its communications?

Netnography may also be able to discover:

1/ Ways to better display consumers' interests on the company website
2/ How to modify the company website to meet changes due to seasonal variations, special events (Super Bowl, Olympic Games, Cricket World Cup, etc.)
3/ Modify or produce new products or services that meet consumers' expressions

---

7   As with all forms of research with human subjects, ethics are vital in netnography. In netnography there is a temptation to hide from online participants and to not disclose your purpose for joining the forum or group. It is not ethical for a researcher, especially one who is employed to conduct the netnography, to remain a hidden observer. A researcher must disclose his or her presence and the overall objectives of the research to the forum or group just as they would in a real world setting.

4/   Refine social media presence and search engine optimization

What are the limitations to netnography?

Practical limitations of netnography

Finding a suitable online forum is usually not a problem. However, with some products or services this may not be the case, and readily accessible well-developed online communities may be difficult to locate, join or observe. In such instances researchers will have to be open-minded and pursue creative methods to identify appropriate online sources.

Cost limitations of netnography

Netnography is a relatively inexpensive form of qualitative consumer research. The main cost arises from the researcher who may need to spend considerable time gathering data or overtly interacting in online forums.

Bias limitations of netnography

The usual caveats for qualitative research apply here. The interpretations of the online behaviours or comments observed by the netnographer will be subjective. This bias may be reduced by employing more than one researcher or by asking other researchers to check interpretations.

Now You

Which site or online forum would you search for netnographic research on your chosen sample product or service? What kinds of information do you hope to collect there?

Further reading

Bortree, D.S. (2005) Presentation of Self on the Web: An Ethnographic Study of Teenage Girls' Weblogs, *Education, Communication & Information* 5(1): 25–39.

Buchanan, E.A. (ed.) (2003) *Virtual Research Ethics: Issues and Controversies,* Hershey, PA, Idea Group Publishing.

Buchanan, E.A. (2000) Ethics, qualitative research, and ethnography in virtual space, *Journal of Information Ethics* 9(2): 82–87.

Davies, C.A. (2007) *Reflexive Ethnography: A Guide to Researching Selves and Others*, (The ASA Research Methods) London: Routledge.

Horst, H.A., & Miller. D. (eds.) (2012) *Digital Anthropology*, London: Bloomsbury Academic.

Boellstorff, T., Nardi, B. Peace, C., and Taylor, T.L. (2012) *Ethnography and Virtual Worlds: A Handbook of Method*, Princeton. NJ: Princeton University Press.

Halfpenny, P., and Proctor, R. (eds.) (2015) *Innovations in Digital Research Methods*, Thousand Oaks, CA: Sage.

Hine, C.M. (2000) *Virtual Ethnography*, Thousand Oaks, CA: Sage.

Hine, C.M. (2005) *Virtual Methods*. London: Bloomsbury Academic.

Kozinets, R.V. (2009) *Netnography: Doing Ethnographic Research Online*, Thousand Oaks, CA: Sage.

Kozinets, R.V. (2015) *Netnography: Redefined*, Thousand Oaks, CA: Sage.

Miller, D., and Slater, D. (2001) *The Internet: An Ethnographic Approach*, London: Bloomsbury Academic.

Markham, A.M. (1998). *Life Online: Researching Real Experience in Virtual Space*, London, Sage.

Miller, D. (2011) *Tales from Facebook*, Oxford: Polity Press.

Richelieu, A., and Bernard K. (2014) The consumption experience of Tim Hortons' coffee fans, *Qualitative Market Research: An International Journal*, *17*(3), p. 192–208. DOI: 10.1108/QMR-06-2012-0032

Simone, G., La Rocca, A., Mandelli, A., and Snehota, I. (2014) Netnography Approach as a Tool for Marketing Research: the case of Dash-P&G/TTV, *Management Decision*, *52*(4) p. 689–704.

Underberg, N.M., and Zorn, E. (2014) *Digital Ethnography: Anthropology, Narrative, and New Media*, Austin: University of Texas Press.

Chapter 9. Visual Ethnography

What is visual ethnography?

Visual consumer ethnography is essentially the collection of two-dimensional images in order to: tell a story about a product or service; locate a product or a service within its usage community; present details when interviews, textual or other forms of information are not available; and to provide uniquely rich visual information free from the distortion that comes from describing an activity. A visual ethnographical study involves the collection and presentation of appropriately selected graphic materials.

Visual ethnography, an approach that employs photography, video or hypermedia as research tools, is a relatively new method utilized in consumer settings (see Schwartz, 1989, for an early and thorough example of the use of visual ethnography). Photographs and other visual media have unique properties and communicate information in an inimitable manner that may be applied alone or with other forms of ethnographic enquiry. In particular, these types of images are able to articulate aspects of socio-cultural continuity within communities and offer insights into how these have changed over time and have been influenced by diverse factors. Visual approaches to both ethnography and anthropology have grown in usage since the advent of inexpensive easy-to-use digital cameras, both still and video. Visual ethnography concerns itself with the ways in which graphic materials may link to wider cultural and societal characteristics.

Deep metaphors and visual ethnography.

Within the area of visual ethnography we also include the concept of deep metaphor and the work of Gerald Zaltman and his metaphor extraction approach, the Zaltman Metaphor Elicitation Technique, or ZMET (Zaltman and Zaltman, 2008). ZMET attempts to elicit from participants conscious and sub-conscious motives, thoughts and reasoning about products and services. To accomplish this, the participant is asked to supply a series of images (usually photographs from magazines, etc.) that he or she associates with a product or service. The collected photos may relate to the product or service in any way the respondent wishes but must not be depictions of the product or service itself. This carefully chosen selection of images is then discussed with a researcher who, with the direct help of the participant, arranges the images in a way that is meaningful to the respondent. Essentially, the result of this exercise is a collage that represents a respondent's thoughts and feelings about a product or service. The researcher and participant then have a protracted discussion in order to discover why particular images were included and arranged as they were and to reveal the deep metaphors that underlie the subjects' assembled collage.

What questions does visual ethnography answer?

Visual ethnographies answer questions about naturally occurring behaviours associated with a product or service and about the implicit meaning that products and services have for respondents. These questions are answered in a visually symbolic, though not linguistic, manner.

What are the limitations to visual ethnography?

Practical limitations to visual ethnography

Finding the correct or appropriate materials for your visual ethnography project may be problematic but can usually be resolved.

If the researcher selects the images for the discussion he or she may be conveying a narrative that distorts the consumer's/user's own story. Therefore it may be more appropriate for the consumers to collect and assemble their own visual ethnographies.

Cost limitations to visual ethnography

There are no particular costs associated with visual ethnography over the cost of employing a researcher.

Software may be needed if the researcher and respondent decide they will digitally manipulate the respondent's images to create a collage or form another type of visual ethnography.

Bias limitations to visual ethnography

A visual ethnography is usually a single person's, or a single group of people's, choice of images and the images chosen will inevitably be particular and reflect a narrowly defined perspective. This form of bias (the fact that the findings from the enquiry cannot be generalized beyond the respondents who have completed the research task to other people) is common to all qualitative research and is also the strength of qualitative research (the fact that the findings are personally chosen images with rich personal meanings to the participant and are indicative of an individual's viewpoint rather than a diluted or aggregate, nomothetic perspective).

Now You

In which way can you incorporate visual ethnography into your research project? How would you select the set of images from which the participant is to choose – or would you leave the selection to your subjects? Why?

Further reading

Brown, C., Costley, C., Friend, L., and Varey, R. (2010) Capturing their dream: Video diaries and minority consumers, *Consumption Markets & Culture*, *13*(4), p. 419–436.

Collier, J., and Collier, M. (1986) *Visual Anthropology: Photography as a Research Method*, Albuquerque: University of New Mexico Press.

Davies, C.A. (2007) *Reflexive Ethnography: A Guide to Researching Selves and Others*, (The ASA Research Methods) London: Routledge.

El Guindi, F. (2004) *Visual anthropology: essential method and theory*, Walnut Creek, Calif and Oxford: AltaMira Press.

Fenge, L-A., and Jones, K. (2012) Gay and Pleasant Land? Exploring Sexuality, Ageing and Rurality in a Multi-Method, Performative Project, *British Journal of Social Work*, *42*(2), pp. 300–317.

Freeman, A. (2014) *Metaphor 128 Success Secrets: 128 Most Asked Questions On Metaphor - What You Need To Know*, Newstead, Australia: Emereo Publishing.

Geissel, S. (2012) *Creating Breakthrough Innovations at Consumer Packaged Goods Companies*. Raleigh, NC: Lulu.com.

Gillárová, K.S., Tejkalová, A.N., and Láb, F. (2014) The Undressed Newsroom: The application of visual ethnography in media research, *Journalism Practice*, *8*(5), p. 607–618.

Goffin, K., and Lemke, F. (2010) *Identifying Hidden Needs: Creating Breakthrough Products*, Basingstoke: Palgrave Macmillan.

Kaden, R.J., Linda, G.L., and Prince, M. (2011) *Leading Edge Marketing Research: 21st-Century Tools and Practices*, Thousand Oaks, CA: Sage Publications, Inc.

Kim, D., and Li, X.R. (2013) Introduction to the special issue on advancing research methods in marketing: Editorial, *Journal of Business Research*, *66*(9), pp. 1243–1244.

Mitchell, C. (2011) *Doing Visual Research*, Thousand Oaks, CA: Sage Publications, Inc.

Oh, S. (2012) Photofriend: creating visual ethnography with refugee children *Area*, *44*(3), pp. 382–288.

Pink, S. (2013) *Doing Visual Ethnography*, Thousand Oaks, CA: Sage Publications, Inc.

Pink, S. (2015) *Doing Sensory Ethnography*, Thousand Oaks, CA: Sage Publications, Inc.

Rakic, T., and Chambers, D. (2009) Researcher with a Movie Camera: Visual Ethnography in the Field. *Current Issues in Tourism*, *12*(3), 255–70.

Rakic, T. and Chambers, D. (2012). *An Introduction to Visual Research Methods in Tourism*, London: Routledge.

Schembri, S., and Boyle, M.V. (2013) Visual ethnography: Achieving rigorous and authentic interpretations, *Journal of Business Research, 66*(9), pp. 1251–1254.

Schwartz, D. (1989) Visual Ethnography: Using Photography in Qualitative Research, *Qualitative Sociology, 12*(2), 119–154.

Spencer, S. (2011) *Visual research methods in the social sciences: awakening visions,* London ; New York : Routledge.

Tinkler, P. (2013) Using Photographs in Social and Historical Research, Thousand Oaks, CA: Sage Publications, Inc.

van Marrewijk, A., and Broos, M. (2012) Retail stores as brands: performances, theatre and space, *Consumption Markets & Culture, 15*(4), p. 374–391.

Zaltman, G., and Zaltman, L.H. (2008) *Marketing Metaphoria: What Deep Metaphors Reveal About the Minds of Consumers,* Cambridge, MA: Harvard Business Review Press.

Chapter 10. Artefacts

What are artefacts?

Also spelt artifact, an artefact may best be understood as an item, object, or relic that has been made by human beings and is viewed as possessing historical interest or significance. Artefacts are also seen as providing information about the culture of the people who made or used the artefactual object. Thus, this form of research conducts enquiries into objects with the express aim of revealing the material culture of the subject of your study[8]. Artefacts are usually created as items to serve a practical purpose within a given society in a specific era. When these items are added to other forms of qualitative research, they provide a tangible, physical component to the social understanding that research seeks to convey.

As with all other forms of qualitative consumer research, artefactual studies aim to enhance a company's knowledge of various aspects of consumers' usage of their contemporary or future products. However, at first glance artefactual research does not seem to be directly concerned with these aims. Furthermore, if consumer artefacts are taken out of context, they may either convey very little meaning or may even communicate an incorrect message about the product, service or concept.

It is important to make note about several features of any artefact, for instance: who created the artefact, when was it created, and why? Answers to these questions provide information for understanding the artefact and the consumers' preferences, life-styles, homes, work, celebrations, and recreation.

The following examples will better explain how the term 'artefact' is used in consumer research.

Example 1: The cultural significance of a particular beverage

Artefact: A series of images from advertising posters for a beverage showing idealized usage of the product within social settings over the specific timescale covered by the posters

---

8   Material culture is made up of the physical objects including household tools and articles that provide evidence of the nature of a culture or social grouping.

Questions   The types of questions that may be answered by the posters (artefact) include:

1/ In what settings was the beverage drunk?
2/ Was the beverage consumed socially or alone?
3/ In which specific social situations was the drink offered and consumed

From these three questions arise further questions:

1/ From these images – is it possible to come to any conclusions about specific consumer segments as they relate to the beverage such as: gender, age, socio-economic class, etc.?
2/ What, if any, conclusions can be made about the product and different cultures?

Example 2: The ways in which health care is provided in a community health setting

Artefact: The medical charts that community nurses use when they are planning and delivering care to the general public (nurses may structure these charts and utilize them differently for each patient and /or doctor)

Questions   The questions that may be answered by the posters (artefacts) include:

1/ Who provides what care and to which patients?
2/ Where and when is this provided?
3/ Which medications does each nurse use?
4/ How do practitioners organize their time and work?
5/ Is the care given palliative, preventative, and/or curative?

These two examples provide suggestions for the types of information and understanding that can be produced in a research setting using artefacts. The form of artefactual materials can vary greatly in the ways in which they are used and the answers or insights they produce.

In commercial ethnography and qualitative consumer research the term artefacts is understood to be the collection of 'things' that shed light upon the product or service in which we have an interest. In traditional anthropology the gathering of artefacts meant collecting together physical items that were of cultural significance. This too is our task in the commercial sector. However, rather than gathering religious objects or other items that may have a significant value to the host culture, commercial consumer artefact research assembles objects that are often considered waste products with little or no value (such as packaging materials, etc.).

For example, a researcher who is interested in a certain beverage may collect different beverage containers produced by the manufacturer at different times of year. Consumers throw these artefacts away but these discarded items may display a brand logo along with seasonally specific images and text printed on the exterior of the beverage container. This promotion can provide insight into the positioning of the artefact within the rest of the café's product range, across different times of the year, or in contrast to other manufacturers' beverage containers, etc. In British public houses beer mats (or coasters) are 10 centimetre cardboard mats printed with colourful images and text associated with a specific drink sold in the establishment. These are artefacts, which indicate the positioning of these beers within the market of the local consumer, and suggest the cultural relevance or location of that product.

One point that needs to be made at this time is that there is an overlap between the information and data that is gathered from artefacts, archives, and visual ethnography.

However, visual ethnography gathers visual images to tell a story, archival research assembles materials about the product or service and the relationship of this to consumers, whilst artefactual research typically brings together physical entities or objects which may indirectly inform the researcher's question regarding the cultural significance of the product or service.

What questions do artefacts answer?

Artefacts usually provide us with information about our products or services' historical or contemporary usage and cultural impact or relevance within the culture that is of interest to our research. By inspecting artefacts we are able to compare, for example, differences in historical and contemporary packaging or adverts used for promotion. We are also able to make similar comparisons between different manufacturers' packaging at the same point in time. Carefully chosen artefacts can help add richness to our understanding of the culture that surrounds our product or service.

What are the limitations to artefactual research?

Practical limitations to artefactual research

It may be easy to locate artefacts that relate to our product but it is considerably more difficult to find and bring together artefacts that are directly relevant to our research questions.

Cost limitations to artefactual research

Artefacts in consumer research are often the parts of a product that are disposed of in the consumption of the item. If this is the case then costs may be minimal or may not exist at all.

Bias limitations to artefactual research

Interpretation bias is present when a researcher attempts to attach cultural meaning or significance to an artefact.

Humans are prone to bias and distortion as a result of not being aware of their own era's influence upon their outlook. This form of bias in outlook may be especially acute when contemporary researchers interpret an historical artefact.

Now You

Where would you look for artefacts related to your product or service of interest? How would you assemble these artefacts or pictures of these artefacts? Which of these artefacts are more or less relevant to your specific research question?

Further reading

Ahuvia, A. C. (2005). Beyond the Extended Self: Loved Objects and Consumers' Identity Narratives, *Journal of Consumer Research, 32*(1), 171–84.

Bardhi, F., Eckhardt, G.M., and Arnould, E.J. (2012) Liquid Relationship to Possessions, *Journal of Consumer Research, 39*(3), pp. 510–529.

Berger, A.A. (2010) *The objects of affection: semiotics and consumer culture,* Basingstoke : Palgrave Macmillan.

Boradkar, P. (2010) *Designing things: a critical introduction to the culture of objects,* Oxford: Berg.

Chamblis, D.F., and Schutt, R.K. (2015) *Making Sense of the Social World: Methods of Investigation,* Thousand Oaks, CA: Sage Publications, Inc.

Gregory, K. (1982) Determining the 'consumer object', *Applied Ergonomics, 13*(1), pp. 11–13.

He, L., Cong, F., Liu, Y., and Zhou, X. (2010) The pursuit of optimal distinctiveness and consumer preferences, *Scandinavian Journal of Psychology, 51*(5), pp. 411–417.

Lee, R. (2000) *Unobtrusive Methods In Social Research,* (Understanding Social Research) Milton Keynes: Open University Press.

Merriam, S.B. (2009) *Qualitative Research: A Guide to Design and Implementation,* New York: Jossey-Bass.

Mitchell, C. *(2011) Doing Visual Research,* Thousand Oaks, CA: Sage Publications, Inc.

Eric J. Arnould, Linda L. Price, and Carolyn F.Curasi, 1999, "Cherished Possessions," *Anthropology Newsletter*, (February), 17–18.

Silverman, D. (2001) *Interpreting Qualitative Data*, (2nd Edition). Thousand Oaks, CA: Sage Publications.

Silverman, D. (ed.) (2010) *Qualitative Research*, Thousand Oaks, CA: Sage Publications, Inc.

Tian, K., and Belk, R. (2005) Extended Self and Possessions in the Workplace, *Journal of Consumer Research, 32*(2), pp.297-310.

Webb, E.J., Campbell, D.T. Schwartz, R.D., and Sechrest, L. (1999) *Unobtrusive Measures*, (Sage Classics) Thousand Oaks, CA: Sage Publications, Inc.

Zwick, D., and Dholakia, N. (2006) The Epistemic Consumption Object and Postsocial Consumption: Expanding Consumer-Object Theory in Consumer Research, *Consumption Markets & Culture, 9*(1), p. 17–43.

Chapter 11. Archives

What is archival research?

Archive is a term that is usually understood to mean a collection of documents or other materials, which are historical in nature and provide information about places, people, and their activities. An archive is also an accumulation of records and the physical place where historical documents are stored. In computing, an archive has a similar connotation, as it is typically a device external to the computer, upon which less frequently accessed information, often in large quantities, is stored. In consumer research, the term archive is best understood as the finding and evaluating of relevant documents or texts leading to a systematic interpretation of the stored material. The documents that have been explored within a piece of archival research may be further analysed through additional research, i.e. by making comparisons across time or place which may then provide an alternative understanding of the material. Additionally, archival research allows investigators to question and/or support existing research and to unite results for separate sources within a broader context (Corti, 2004).

More specifically, in the context of consumer research, archives can best be thought of as being materials that have been printed, filmed, audio recorded or in some other way documented. These archives form a body of information about a product or a service that may supply valuable details about consumer usage of or responses to products and services.

In addition archives provide records about product or service development, modification, and pricing, most often within an historical context. Archives may contain primary source materials that have been collected by a manufacturer, retailer, wholesaler, etc., and demonstrate the life history of the person, organization, service or item that they are documenting. Archives often contain legal and commercial information.

Because of their documentary nature, the contents of an archive are selected to create a chosen historical narrative. **Unlike books, archival material is normally unpublished and usually unique. Companies may keep an archive of their activities or products** (for example, Coca-Cola). Governments (national and local) also maintain archives, which can yield interesting information. Web archives perform a similar function for information that has appeared on the World Wide Web.

According to Smith and Lux (1993) historical archives offer a qualitative interpretive approach, which alone can explain antecedents and changes over time. Therefore, archives have the potential to increase our understanding of volatile and changing consumer situations. However, it should be noted that archival research is not as widely used as some of the other methods of consumer research mentioned in this book.

What questions does archival research answer?

Some examples of enquiries that may be addressed through archival research are: what is the history of this product or service; how has this product or service developed since a particular date; or over a given period; how has this product or service fared in its competitive market during a certain span of time?

What are the limitations of archival research?

Practical limitations of archival research

The archival material that is available to you may not focus on the specific question(s) you are asking in your research. Archival material is generally historical in nature and therefore may not address your product or service, as it exists in the contemporary market. If you are looking at material contained in a very large archive, you may find research painstaking, time consuming, and costly. Rather than directly answer your research questions, archival research is most likely to produce background information for your research project.

Cost limitations of archival research

Archival research is labour intensive as it may involve looking through a lot of potential materials that are not relevant to your specific enquiries. Due to the enormity of undertaking some types of archival research, the approach is a relatively costly procedure and may produce little information for the cost involved.

Bias limitations of archival research

Archives have usually been assembled by someone or some organization and may incorporate a bias in the very act of data collection and retention. Thus, the collection process is almost inevitably selective and most often introduces some sort of bias. Furthermore, only certain materials remain within an archive over time and this discriminating process is also an invitation for potential bias.

Now You

What kind of archival material might help you answer the research question about your product or service? Where do you think you could find such material?

Further reading

Bell, S.S. (2015) *Librarian's Guide to Online Searching: Cultivating Database Skills for Research and Instruction*, Santa Barbara, AC: Libraries Unlimited.

Chamblis, D.F., and Schutt, R.K. (2015) *Making Sense of the Social World: Methods of Investigation*, Thousand Oaks, CA: Sage Publications, Inc.

Corti, L. (2004) Archival Research, in Lewis-Beck, M.S., Bryman, A., and Liao, T.F. (2004) *The Sage Encyclopedia of Social Science Research Methods*. DOI: http://dx.doi.org/10.4135/9781412950589.

Dunn, D.S. (2012) *Research Methods for Social Psychology*, New York: Wiley.

Gottschalk, L. (2006) The Historian and the Historical Documents, in Scott, J. (ed.) *Documentary Research: Vol. I*, (pp. 43–82). London: Sage.

Halls, P. (2010) Pros and cons of online archive data for academic research, *The Journal for the Serials Community, 23*(3), pp. 222–225.

Hock, R. (2013) *The Extreme Searcher's Internet Handbook: A Guide for the Serious Searcher*, Medford Township, NJ: Information Today, Inc.

Hughes, J. (2014) *Documentary and Archival Research*, London: Sage.

Leedecker, C.H. (1991) *Historical Dimensions in Consumer Research, Historical Archaeology, 25*(2), pp. 30–45.

Mann, T (2015) The Oxford Guide to Library Research, Oxford: Oxford University Press.

Smallwood, C. (2015) *The Complete Guide to Using Google in Libraries: Research, User Applications, and Networking* (Volumes 1 and 2), Lanham, MD: Rowman & Littlefield Publishers.

Smith, R.A., and Lux, D.S. (1993) Historical Method in "Consumer Research: Developing Causal Explanations of Change, *Journal of Consumer Research, 19*(4). 595–610.

Strasser, S. (2003) The Alien Past: Consumer Culture in Historical Perspective, *Journal of Consumer Policy, 26*(4), pp. 375–393.

Taylor, M., and Mitchell, J, (2015) Google in Special Collections and Archives, in, Smallwood, C. (ed.) *The Complete Guide to Using Google in Libraries: Research, User Applications, and Networking (Volume 2)*, Lanham, MD: Rowman & Littlefield Publishers. p. 123–132.

Tesar, M. (2015) Ethics and Truth in Archival research, *History of Education, 44*(1), p. 101–114.

Chapter 12. Journals and Diaries

What are journals?

Journals, journaling, blogging, video journals, diaries, etc., are all descriptive of this class of qualitative research approach. In this guide book we will typically call this group of techniques diary keeping or journaling and only refer to other specific approaches of this genre when these are distinguished from the general approach discussed below.

What questions do journals answer?

When asking consumers to fill in a questionnaire, complete an in-depth interview, or take part in a focus group, etc., researchers often rely upon consumers' accurate recall of their behaviours. The act of journaling also relies upon memory but can sometimes mitigate effects of poor recall. By asking respondents to complete a diary, at the time of, or soon after an activity (such as purchasing), or while they are engaging in an activity (such as the usage of a product), the accuracy of the respondents thoughts and feelings about an item will often be more precise than when recall over time is involved. These diaries or journals can be created as a paper diary, on a smart phone or handheld device. Alternately, some research companies have developed specific hardware such as handheld devices that are solely used to gather this data and loan these units to respondents for the duration of a project.

What are the limitations of journals?

Practical limitations of journals

Finding respondents may be problematic, as they will have to meet several criteria in order to participate. For example, if the focus of a project is the reactions of experienced consumers of a particular product, then the researcher will want to find participants who are highly informed about the product. Conversely, investigations requiring the documentation of novice responses to a product or service will require a neophyte's impressions of an item. Respondents must also have the motivation and time available to undertake a lengthy, time-consuming, diary keeping exercise.

Cost limitations of journals

Diaries or journals may require the person keeping the journal to make frequent entries over a protracted period of time. Due to the prolonged and in-depth nature of participant involvement, the incentives that a research team needs to provide for journal completion may be costly. Other expenses involve the production or preparation of the diaries themselves (either on-line, digital, or physical), as well as the distribution of the diaries before and their collection after the study period. In addition, analyses of the diaries' extensive free-text and assorted images may become costly.

Bias limitations of journals

Biases in diary keeping often stem from the researcher imposing an inhibitive constraint upon a consumer's purchasing activity or other related pursuits. Not only does journaling require a lengthy time investment but also the activity requests consumers to overtly record behaviours that they might prefer to keep hidden. Potential difficulties and inaccuracies may also arise when participants feel obligated to fill in their entries and write 'anything' that comes to mind, simply in order to fill in the required space in their diaries, thus effecting the authenticity of the data gathered.

Another potential bias may be introduced when participants are asked to mull over their actions, beliefs, feelings, etc., about a product or service. Here too, participants may be tempted to make up explanations, for instance, by stating a certain reason for buying a particular product, when in fact the behaviour was habitual and less thoughtful than they would like to admit.

Now You

What kinds or parts of your research questions may journaling help to answer? Which type of journal (paper, digital, …) would you ask your participants to use?

Further reading

Alaszewski, A.M. (2006) *Using Diaries for Social Research,* (Introducing Qualitative Methods series) Thousand Oaks, CA: Sage Publications, Inc.

Bolger, N., and Laurenceau, J-P. (2013) *Intensive Longitudinal Methods: An Introduction to Diary and Experience Sampling Research,* (Methodology in the Social Sciences) New York: The Guilford Press.

Braun, V., and Clarke, V. (2013) *Successful Qualitative Research: A Practical Guide for Beginners,* Thousand Oaks, CA: Sage Publications, Inc.

Dunn, D.S. (2012) *Research Methods for Social Psychology,* New York: Wiley.

Etherington, K. (2004). *Becoming reflexive researchers: Using ourselves in research,* London: Jessica Kingley.

Kremenitzer, J. P. (2005). The Emotionally Intelligent Early Childhood Educator: Self-Reflective Journaling. *Early Childhood Education Journal, 33,* 3–9.

Livholts, M., and Tamboukou, M. (2015) *Discourse and Narrative Methods: Theoretical Departures, Analytical Strategies and Situated Writings,* Thousand Oaks, CA: Sage Publications, Inc.

Malacrida, C. (2007) Reflexive Journaling on Emotional Research Topics: Ethical Issues for Team Researchers, *Qualitative Health Research, 17;* 1329–1339. DOI: 10.1177/1049732307308948

Mruck, K., & Breuer, F. (2003, May). Subjectivity and reflexivity in qualitative research-The FQS issues. *Forum Qualitative Sozialforschung, 4*(2). Retrieved, from http://www.qualitative-research.net/index.php/fqs/article/view/696/1505

Nezlek, J.B. (2012) *Diary Methods,* (The SAGE Library of Methods in Social and Personality Psychology) Thousand Oaks, CA: Sage Publications, Inc.

Ortlipp, M. (2008) Keeping and Using Reflective Journals in the Qualitative Research Process, *The Qualitative Report,* 13(4), 695–705. http://www.nova.edu/ssss/QR/QR13-4/ortlipp.pdf

Richardson, L. (1994). Writing: A Method of Inquiry. In N. Denzin (Ed.), *Handbook of Qualitative Research,* (pp. 516–529). Thousand Oaks, CA: Sage.

Tillman, L. C. (2003). Mentoring, Reflection, and Reciprocal Journaling. *Theory Into Practice, 42,* 226–233.

Chapter 13. Autoethnography

What is autoethnography?

The word autoethnography is a blend of the word 'ethnography,' meaning the systematically undertaken description of cultures and individuals and their customs, with 'auto' which, when placed before another word, means self. An autoethnography is a self-ethnography conducted by ethnographers themselves concerning their own behaviours, reactions, and beliefs. In the context of consumer ethnography this will take the form of the autoethnographer's use, purchase, maintenance, evaluation, etc., of the service or product that is of interest to the research project.

Autoethnography is a research method, which connects a researcher's personal story, including broader cultural meanings and political and social understandings, with the researcher's first-hand experiences through a process of self-reflection and writing[9]. To put this another way: the cultural significance of a person's experiences are described and systematically analysed within an autoethnography through a process of writing a focused and specified individual account. Indeed, in an autoethnography the process of keeping a diary is often seen as a way for the person who is writing the diary to discover what they know about something, in our case a product, service or concept. Given this process of self-discovery, an autoethnography and its revelatory nature can be seen to be both a product and a process (see for example: Ellis, 2004; Holman-Jones, 2005). Autoethnography has its own strengths and weaknesses yet challenges notions of the researcher as someone who conducts research upon others (Adams & Holman-Jones, 2008, Spry, 2001) by being a procedure in which the researcher is his or her own subject of study.

"The autoethnographer is simultaneously the subject and the object of the research, observing and interpreting culture through reflecting on his or her personal life experiences" (Moisander and Valtonen, p.63). An autoethnography is an autobiography that looks at how the autobiographer is immersed within a culture and carrying out cultural practices. In an attempt to learn about the effects of a culture upon its members, autoethnographers become members themselves and join in with associated cultural practices within their everyday activities. From this standpoint, the researcher undertakes to observe him- or herself. The autoethnographic approach aims to provide insight into how the market produces and sustains the cultural significance and meanings of consumer behaviours.

---

9   The ethnographic approach is akin to the process of reflection upon personal experiences that researchers generally go through at the start of most research projects.

What questions does autoethnography answer?

By situating an ethnographic researcher within the research situation as a user or purchaser of a service or product (a respondent), the researcher is inevitably aware of the research questions, research procedures, client demands, and is able to reflect upon his own consumer experiences. Because an autoethnographer intimately understands the product, client, etc., such a person is uniquely positioned to be able to supply information that will be of direct relevance to client's needs.

What are the limitations to autoethnography?

Practical limitations to autoethnography

The major limitation of autoethnography is also its greatest strength: Because the researcher conducts the autoethnographic procedure, inevitable biases arise in both the management of the fieldwork and the analysis of the arising data.

Cost limitations to autoethnography

Autoethnography requires a single experimenter/respondent to complete the procedure. This person also designs the course of action and analyses the resultant data and whilst this person is highly trained and expensive, the expense is mitigated by the fact that no other personnel need be employed.

Bias limitations to autoethnography

Participant bias is the main, and ever present, weakness of autoethnography. Many researchers query whether it is indeed possible for a researcher to disengage his or her biases and provide impartial information.

In general, as with other sole-respondent research, it is difficult if not impossible to extend the insight gained from the individual participant to other people.

Now You

Do you think it would be difficult or easy for you to perform an autoethnography with regard to your chosen sample product or service? Why? How would you try to control the possible bias of your expectations interfering with your self-observation?

Further reading

Adams, T.E., Holman, S., and Ellis, C. (2014) *Autoethnography,* Understanding Qualitative Research, Oxford: Oxford University Press.

Adams, T.E., & Holman-Jones, S. (2008). Autoethnography is queer, in Denzin, N.K., Lincoln, Y.S., & Smith, L.T. (eds.), *Handbook of critical and indigenous methodologies,* (pp. 373–390). Thousand Oaks, CA: Sage.

Berger, L. (2001) Inside Out: Narrative Autoethnography as a Path Toward Rapport, *Qualitative Inquiry, 7,* 504–518.

Boylorn, R.M., and Orbe, M.P. (eds.) (2013) *Critical Autoethnography: Intersecting Cultural Identities in Everyday Life* (Writing Lives) Walnut Creek, CA: Left Coast Press.

Buzard, J. (2003) On Auto-Ethnographic Authority, *The Yale Journal of Criticism, 16*(1), 61–91.

Chang, H. (2009) *Autoethnography as Method,* (Developing Qualitative Inquiry) Walnut Creek, CA: Left Coast Press.

Chang, H., Ngunjiri, F., and Hernandez, K-A.C. (2012) *Collaborative Autoethnography (Developing Qualitative Inquiry)* Walnut Creek, CA: Left Coast Press.

Chin, E. (2007) The Consumer Diaries, or, Autoethnography in the Inverted World, *Journal of Consumer Culture, 7* (3), 335–353. doi: 10.1177/1469540507081628

Denzin, N.K. (2013) *Interpretive Autoethnography,* (Qualitative Research Methods) Thousand Oaks, CA: Sage Publications, Inc.

Ellis, C. (2004). *The ethnographic I: A methodological novel about autoethnography,* Walnut Creek, CA: AltaMira Press.

Etherington, K. (2004) *Becoming Reflexive Researchers: Using Ourselves in Research,* London: Jessica Kingley.

Gatson, S.N. (2003) On Being Amorphous: Autoethnography, Genealogy, and a Multiracial Identity, *Qualitative Inquiry, 9,* 20–48.

Gould, S. J. (2012) The Emergence of Consumer Introspection Theory (CIT): Introduction to a JBR Special Issue. *Journal of Business Research, 65,* 453–460.

Guzik, E. (2013) Representing Ourselves in Information Science Research: A Methodological Essay on Autoethnography. *Canadian Journal of Information and Library Sciences, 37 (4),* 267–283.

Holman-Jones, S. (2005). Autoethnography: Making the personal political, in Denzin, N.K., Lincoln, Y.S., (eds.), *Handbook of qualitative research,* (pp. 763–791). Thousand Oaks, CA: Sage.

Holt, N.L. (2003) Representation, Legitimation, and Autoethnography: An Autoethnographic Writing Story, *International Journal of Qualitative Methods, 2*(1), 1–22.

Jones, S.H., Adams, T.E., and Ellis, C. (eds.) (2015) *Handbook of Autoethnography,* Walnut Creek, CA: Left Coast Press.

Keenan, J., and Evans, A. (2014) The Use of Estrangement Autoethnography in Higher Education Teaching, *Worcester Journal of Learning and Teaching, 9,* 1–10.

Martineau, J. (2001) Autoethnography and Material Culture: The Case of Bill Reid. *Biography, 24*(1), 242–258.

Minowa, Y., Maclaran, P., and Visconti, L. (2010) Tales of Invisible Cities: Methodological Avenues For Multi-Sited Researcher Autoethnography, in Campbell, M.C., Inman, J., and Pieters, R. (eds.) *Advances in Consumer Research, 37,* Duluth, MN: Association for Consumer Research, 680–681.

Moisander, J., and Valtoner, A. (2006) *Qualitative Marketing Research: A Cultural Approach,* Thousand Oaks, CA: Sage Publications, Inc.

Muncey, T. (2005) Doing Autoethnography. *International Journal of Qualitative Methods.* 4(1), 1–12.

Muncey, T. (2010) *Creating Autoethnographies,* Thousand Oaks, CA: Sage Publications, Inc.

Pellas, R.J. (2003) The Academic Tourist: An Autoethnography, *Qualitative Inquiry.* 9, 369–373.

Reed-Danahay, D. (1997). *Auto/Ethnography: Rewriting the self and the social.* New York: Berg.

Spry, T. (2001). Performing autoethnography: An embodied methodological praxis. *Qualitative Inquiry, 7*(6), 706–732.

Section 3 – Practical Procedures

Introduction

At the heart of qualitative research is the notion that the human researcher is the "measuring device" that extracts and brings forth the research evidence. The manner in which this is achieved is certainly an intricate process with all sorts of ontological and epistemological questions about the human mind and about inter-subjectivity. Thus, qualitative research is something we do every day (observing and relating to others, creating and extracting interpersonal meaning, etc.). Within the present consumer research context this process is, to a certain degree institutionalized, and thus "professionalized" to be part of positive science.

This third section contains instructions on ways to conduct qualitative consumer behaviour research and is arranged using the same chapter themes as in section one. It should be noted that the specific aim of this book is to be a concise introduction to the methods presented in a taught course in qualitative consumer research. Ideally, this text may supplement an in-depth reading of the textbook Qualitative Methods in Consumer Psychology: Ethnography and Culture (Hackett, 2015). The instructions in this section refer to ways to conduct a series of practice procedures with the specific purpose of exposing you *how* to undertake each technique. Consequently, the procedures may not translate perfectly to the field or real world setting. For instance, in this book it is suggested that a focus group interview should take approximately 20–30 minutes. Whereas, a real world focus group is rarely this short and typically is 90–120 minutes in length. The reason for the abbreviated nature of this taught exercise is that generally it would be impossible to have the time or resources for students to conduct a series of two-hour-long focus groups. Perhaps more importantly, we have observed that 20 minutes is enough time for students to appreciate the principles and ideas behind the focus group activity, to identify what worked and what did not, and to be able to make suggestions as to how the session could be improved. Focus groups that last longer than this tend to be confusing. It is a lot to expect of a novice at moderating to preside successfully over a focus group for one to two hours. Likewise, the participants in student focus groups do not receive the incentives that commercially sponsored researchers are able to provide and the topics in a course setting may be less engaging.

As well as focus groups many of the other procedures in this text have been altered from commercial practice in order to make them more appropriate to a learning situation. We will attempt to point out these differences as they occur in their corresponding chapters.

In the previous chapters, you have familiarized yourself with some of the key ideas of the ten research approaches presented in this guide by thinking through the questions asked in the "Now You" sections. In the upcoming chapters, we encourage you to actively engage in planning your research project. Even if you won't actually realize a study, do yourself the favour of being as diligent in following the suggestions as if you were about to conduct the research as a member of a real-life research team.

Chapter 14. Projective Techniques

Outline

Projective techniques, or projectives as they are commonly called, are consumer behaviour research procedures that attempt to unmask the subconscious thoughts, feelings, and beliefs that a product user or customer may have. The techniques described in this section, and how they are utilized, are especially open to modification and innovation due to the procedure's reliance on the creative nature of the participant's responses. All of these approaches aim to subvert conscious filters that respondents may employ when answering questions about their behaviours, beliefs, and motives. Participants often replace veritable answers with more socially acceptable and rationalized ones in an attempt to create a desired or acceptable impression. Of course, such distortion will always be present in any research procedure but projective procedures endeavour to minimize these effects.

Projectives fall into broad classes of procedures, such as: sorts; maps/mapping; completion tasks, etc.

Preparation

Perhaps more than some of the other procedures presented in this book, good projective techniques need to be well planned and thoroughly prepared. The requirement for detailed planning arises mainly from the flexible nature of projective procedures. When using projectives, research teams will have to think carefully about what they are attempting to discover. All research may be biased, for example, a questionnaire may incorporate leading questions. However, projectives are especially prone to bias as respondents are asked to complete creative tasks, which are interpreted by researchers who make inferences about possible relationships between the response and the product or service. Consequently projectives should be well piloted and discussed prior to their usage. You should spend time designing projectives and discussing these within your team.

Location

Projectives may be conducted in a wide variety of locations. Dependent upon the format of the technique, some projectives will need to be performed in specialized settings. For example, creativity walls may be used (large prepared boards, blank walls, etc.) upon which participants are asked to write, draw, etc. However, in student settings the projectives that are most likely to be employed are sort procedures or some form of mapping process. These can be undertaken in any relatively quiet environment with a medium sized flat surface, wall, table or clip-board upon which participants may sort items, paint, draw, write, etc.

Materials

The use of a digital video recorder can greatly enhance the results of projective techniques. To record the sessions, students generally prefer to utilise their phones, which are well suited for the job. Student research teams should have enough members, so that one student will be able to facilitate the procedure while another digitally records the process and others take notes on participant and facilitator behaviour. Remember to obtain permission from participants to allow the recording of their session.

Participants

Projectives attempt to discover the underlying subconscious process of a consumer's motives and other sociological constructs. Consequently, projective techniques are often used with individual participants in an interview type setting, or more commonly, as a sub-component activity within a focus group. When the technique is used, those persons selected must possess appropriate knowledge or experience that relates to the study questions. Details about what constitutes a respondent group or how to recruit focus group participants when projectives are used can be found in Chapter 15 of this guidebook.

Projective techniques should be introduced to participants in a similar manner to any form of marketing research. The researcher or facilitator (i.e., you!) explains the purpose of the study and answers any questions the respondent might have. Once the facilitator has established rapport with the participant(s) he or she introduces the projective procedure in a non-prescriptive manner. By this we mean that a few possible ways for completing a projective task can be suggested but you should emphasize that there are multiple ways to complete the task and none of these are better or worse than any other. You should explain to the participant the steps necessary to finish the projective task rather than tell or demonstrate what the participant should or should not say or do.

For example, when asking a participant to sort objects in a multiple-sort procedure, you ask the participant to arrange the items in **any manner** that the participant feels may indicate relationships between the objects. You should not suggest or demonstrate to the participant how to arrange items in a straight line, into three piles, etc. In table 2 below examples are provided of impartial and biased introductions to projective techniques. In the first two examples the bias is due to the researcher supplying possible responses, which will tend to limit replies to these suggestions. In the third example, as well as providing possible responses, the biased introduction is too verbose and may overwhelm or confuse participants.

Table 2. Introducing a Projective Procedure

Biased introduction	Impartial introduction
Here you have a number of items. You can arrange them in any manner you like, for example, you could form a square, a line or a circle	Here you have a number of items. Would you please arrange them here on the table in any manner that has meaning for you
Please tell me whether you associate positive or negative concepts to this type of car	Please tell me what words come to mind when you look at this car
The stick figure is you. When you go into the store and you are feeling happy or sad, perhaps you are thinking this is a waste of your time, or maybe not. Tell me how you are feeling, thinking and what you want to do	Here is a stick figure. Imagine this is you and you have walked into the store. What are you thinking, feeling and what do you want to do?

There are, however, occasions when the researcher has specific categories or concepts in mind that are related to the product or service. In these instances the facilitator may impose constraints upon the procedure. For example, a research project may be concerned with the influence of price upon a respondent's reactions to a given product. In this instance the researcher may suggest price, or price bands, as a category into which items are then sorted.

As the facilitator, you should adopt the same impartial perspective and approach when you preside over other projective techniques. For example in a mapping exercise, participants may be asked to supply a word, phrase, or concept that is related to a product. Here too, you must display **a neutral manner.** However, in other instances, the facilitator may suggest the type of word, phrase or concept he or she is looking for (in a similar way to the above illustration of price in a sort procedure). Examples of these two approaches are as follows: an impartial manner is required when the facilitator asks a participant to say what comes to mind when presented with the name of a certain beverage. Yet a guiding approach is permissible when questioning the participant more directly about where, when, or with whom the participant makes associations when viewing the named beverage.

Results

Often the output or results from a projective procedure is visual and may take the form of a *sheet of paper* (an artefact) upon which the participant and/or facilitator have drawn and written. In a student setting this sheet of paper may be digital but is more likely notepaper. Whether actual paper or its digital equivalent, the artefact is a significant part of the results as are the facilitator's notes, observers' documentations, and the digital recordings (visual and/or audio) of the procedures: How participants physically complete the set tasks can provide important data about their psychological processes.

Analyses (including thematic analysis)

The artefacts, textual notes, aural and visual documentations of the participant performing the projective procedures will be evaluated and thematically analysed in the same way that results are analysed from other types of qualitative research. This means that you and your team members will examine and re-examine the data several times over in order to identify key issues (themes) and assemble this information into groups of ideas that furnish details to support the topics or themes that were found to emerge from the results. Non-verbal communications, as well as other forms of participant behaviour all contribute to the meaning-making process.

It is useful for two or more researchers to interpret the data independently and then later come together to compare and discuss their findings. As well as reflecting both individually and together upon their analyses, you and your team members may identify good and less good practices, which in turn may be a useful learning technique for investigators. Checking between different researchers' interpretations not only applies to projective techniques but to most other forms of qualitative research.

Chapter 15. Focus Groups

Outline

Matters that need to be considered when conducting a focus group interview include the following:

1/ Costs
2/ Time constraints
3/ Objectives of the research
4/ Determine how the resulting data will be analysed
5/ Choose who the respondents will be
6/ Decide how respondents will be selected

Preparation

Due to the complexity of organizing focus groups, this form of research requires a lot of preparation if it is to be successful. For example: the focus group requires planning in terms of recruiting appropriate participants; deciding on the stimulus materials that are to be used during the session; choosing at least one specialized and trained moderator to conduct the focus group interview procedure; selecting recording equipment and collecting the appropriate forms of written informed consent from participants for the type of recording planned; picking a specialized location which may need to be reserved for a specific time; etc.

Therefore if the focus group is to be successfully undertaken, considerable planning and organization is required.

Location

Focus groups may be conducted in any quiet environment that is large enough to accommodate the number of people involved. Dedicated focus group rooms are often used in commercial market research. These rooms are used solely to conduct focus groups and constitute two rooms that are divided by a two-way mirror. The participants sit in the one room around a table while the moderator and the researchers are in the other room from where they can observe, hear, record and oversee the group process. If this type of facility is unavailable then a classroom may be used.

Materials

A checklist of materials is a good idea since focus groups are complex situations that require good organization. There are specific items that should be included on the checklist that apply to both the moderator and participants.

Materials the moderator requires:

1/ Focus group schedule or discussion guide: an outline or checklist of the main issues to be covered along with sub-probes
2/ List of basic details of the activities that the moderator plans to use
3/ Implements for note taking (pen, pencil, tablet or note book: make sure there are enough pages left in the book)
4/ A flip chart: if you decide to use one
5/ A stand for the flip chart or tape, pins, to fix the chart to a wall
6/ Markers to use on the flip chart
7/ Name tags, badges, name plaques for each respondent that are clearly written with text that can be read by the moderator and other participants from a distance of three or four meters
8/ Recording equipment: video or audio as previously agreed upon with participants, although a mobile phone is usually adequate for focus groups conducted by students
9/ A secondary recording device in case the first device fails
10/ Extension cord for recorder (if needed)
11/ Make sure recording devices are charged, take spare batteries
12/ Consent forms: bring more than the number of respondents attending
13/ A debriefing schedule (a summary of the research project along with details of who students may contact for details of the research findings. This should also include thanks to participants)

Materials for the group:

1/ Stimulus materials (there may be very few or a great many stimulus materials and the research team needs to plan: how this is to be used and when and who will receive these; whether participants will bring any materials or will they be given these, etc.)
2/ Paper, pens, pencils, etc., as needed
3/ Refreshments (food/drink) as needed

Participants

In focus groups the ideal participant is a person who is a super-user of your product or has a specific relationship with your product or service. Respondents are not usually sampled to be representative of a population of users. In some focus groups you may, however, use participants who do not know your product and you may introduce them to the product during the focus group and discuss their reactions. Yet, the aim of a focus group is to bounce ideas around between members of the group and to generate further ideas. Therefore, you should select participants thoughtfully and choose participants who are most likely to come up with the type of information for which you are looking.

This guidebook suggests that if you conduct a focus group as part of a class or just for trying out the procedure, then all participants in a student focus group be fellow class members or people you know. Some of these people will be more suitable to participate in the group than others (e.g., because of their gender, familiarity with a specific product, living on or off campus, etc.). You must develop a profile of the ideal participant for your specific product or service. You and your team members should consider this ideal profile in relation to your study's overall research questions when selecting specific persons for inclusion in the focus group.

Procedure

The procedure for the class-based focus group is as follows.

As the moderator, you must:

1/ Be in the focus group room prior to the respondents' arrival and the commencement of the focus group
2/ Organize the focus group room, materials, chairs, stimulus materials, provide pens, paper, etc., for participants (as needed)
3/ Establish that other members of the research team know what their roles are to be during the session and are positioned correctly inside the focus group room and in the control room. In the control room observers and others may sit unseen and unheard by focus group participants
4/ Plan refreshments
5/ Welcome participants as they arrive into the focus group room and provide a brief explanation of:
 – The purpose of the research in general and the focus group in particular
 – What participants can expect to happen while they are taking part in the focus group procedure
 – What the information collected during the session will be used for: What is/are the goal(s) of the research in general and the focus group in particular. Explanations should be detailed enough to orient the participants' thinking toward the topic at hand, but not so detailed as to guide or cue participants' responses

- Who the moderator is and his or her role in the procedure and introduce anyone else who has a responsibility in the focus group room – i.e., co-moderators, note takers, etc.
- The expected duration of the focus group. The moderator must stress the importance of the respondents' participation throughout the length of the focus group session. HOWEVER: participants must be informed of their rights as research subjects, what participation will entail, and that they may withdraw from the focus group or not answer any question that causes them discomfort at any time at no cost or penalty to themselves
- Why their written consent is needed (i.e. participation on their part and your right to video/audio record the discussion). Ensure that you have received written consent from all participants.
- Location of the nearest bathroom

6/ Become over-familiar with: the research topic; the main aims of the project; any previous results from other research procedures that have been conducted for this study; the questions to be asked during the focus group; who the members of the focus group are and the focus group schedule.

At the end of the focus group, as the moderator, you are obliged to:

7/ Thank participants for their time and participation
8/ Ask participants if they have any final questions and answer these
9/ Ask participants if they would be willing to engage in further research connected with this project. If they are, check to make sure you have their contact details
10/ Provide participants with a name and contact information for the research team if questions or issues about the research arise at a later time
11/ Ensure participants have received payment or reward for their participation if applicable

The moderator and research team must also:

12/ Complete a de-briefing session immediately after the focus group to gather instant responses from all note takers, co-moderators, observers, etc., and take details on their comments and reactions. Do not postpone this activity until a later time as the richness of interactions will fade and even if you don't imagine this to happen, you will quickly forget what you saw and heard.
13/ Label and catalogue all recordings, notes, etc.,
14/ Have a designated person collect and store any hand-written notes, recordings, consent forms, debriefing details, etc. All of these materials must be put away carefully and not allowed into the public domain. This material must be stored in the manner you described

and for the time period you specified in the informed consent document signed by each participant.

Results

The format of the results that arise from your focus group will be that of the field notes taken by those observing the session along with any video and/or audio recordings. Other results that may arise in the form of visual data will be the artefacts that developed out of procedures performed during the focus group, such as a sort technique or a creativity session.

Analyses (including thematic analysis)

The notes, artefacts, projective procedure results, video and audio recordings resulting from the focus group will be evaluated and thematically analysed in the same way that results are analysed from other types of qualitative research as discussed in the previous chapter. Key issues will be identified and assembled into clusters of ideas that support the themes arising from the data. These themes may emerge in responses documented from individual participants as well as from the focus group discussion and reactions as a whole. The analysis stage may also include the gathering of verbatim quotations, which can be then incorporated into the research report and project presentation.

An example may clarify this thematic analysis procedure. For example, imagine you conducted a focus group in order to optimise the interior of a new model of automobile. You noted reactions and innovative suggestions from a number of participants as well as comments from other participants who commented positively on the arrangement of the controls within the automobile interior. The group also discussed the excellent acoustics from the sound system. Furthermore, participants reported that locating the mirror and seat adjustments when travelling in the car for the first time was awkward. The seats were described as comfortable but difficult to remove or collapse if occupants needed extra space.

In this example, one possible set of themes emerging from the focus group may be: spatial layout of driving controls; spatial layout of comfort controls; sound quality; general comfort; positive features; negative features. You can then use these emergent themes as general categories under which you will be able to arrange other more detailed responses and explore the inter-relationships between themes. Furthermore, you may use verbatim quotations or the descriptions of the group's activities to illustrate and expand upon the meaning of the themes you have identified. Verbatim quotations can also authenticate and legitimize "data" so that written up results do not rely upon inferred meaning.

Chapter 16. In-Depth Interviews

Outline

The in-depth interview is a relatively simple technique in qualitative consumer research, however, even though it is ostensibly a structured discussion between a researcher and a participant, there are many things that can go wrong. These mistakes, oversights, etc., can be deleterious to the quality of the data that arises from the strategy.

Preparation

The questions intended to be asked during the procedure are the principal preparations required for the in-depth interview. In a marketing research context an in-depth interview may last one or two hours. However, for this learning procedure, each interview should last between 20 and 30 minutes. You must therefore prepare a series of questions about your sample service or product. These questions will be developed from the findings from research already undertaken as part of your own or the group project, such as literature search and projective procedures. Based upon this information approximately three to five main questions should be devised and each question should have a similar number of follow-up-probe questions.

The location for the interview must be as quiet and distraction free as possible and the note-takers and team members who are video or audio recording the session must be positioned to be as unobtrusive as possible.

Location

When conducted as part of a taught course, in-depth interviews may be conducted in class during regular school hours. If possible, several other classrooms should be utilized in order to minimize the distracting effect that an interview may have upon multiple sessions taking place at the same time.

Materials

Materials for in-depth interviews are minimal. Essential items are: an interview schedule; video/audio recording equipment; notebook; pen/pencil; seating for interviewer and interviewee.

Participants

You may choose any participant from whom you think you can elicit responses relevant to your research questions. In a class setting, students may choose other students from the class to be the respondents in their in-depth interviews. In all cases, in-depth interview participants should be selected because of their knowledge and experience regarding the product, service or concept under research.

Procedure

In order to familiarize yourself with the procedure, you and your team should conduct at least two or three in-depth interviews and each interview should last between 20 and 30 minutes.

Results

In-depth interview results take the form of a video or audio recording of the research interview along with notes that are taken by observers from the research team.

Analyses

After the video/audio recording has been transcribed, you and your research team may begin textual or narrative analysis of the data. As with many other qualitative research approaches texts are read and then re-read in order for the researchers to become 'over-familiar' with the content of the interview. The research team should then attempt to identify themes or issues that emerged during the interview. Also, researchers should note verbatim expressions that they think important within the context of the investigation, which can also authenticate and legitimize the "data." The research team should comment about the unique aspects of the interview as well as its similarities with other interviews and other research procedures. Attempts should be made to interpret these.

The interviewer's role in the in-depth interview should also be analysed. Errors made by the interviewer should be honestly commented upon along with the expected consequences of these transgressions. For example, did the interviewer lead respondents with his or her questioning style or non-verbal communications? In the estimation of the research team, did these infractions significantly affect the research results? What could have been done better, or differently? What impact would the research team expect these types of changes to make on the findings?

Chapter 17. Ethnography

Outline

When we encounter a new environment or situation we often conduct a form of ethnography. For example, a new student may enter a dining hall and carefully monitor other, more experienced students' behaviours, in order to learn about how things are done within this context. In this and in many other situations what is being conducted is a form of ethnographic participant observation.

The ethnographical investigations that you will likely undertake, e.g. as part of a taught course in qualitative consumer research, often takes the form of short-term observation procedures. You will essentially take note of your daily activities in which you encounter other people using your sample service or product. This will not involve any contrivance, as the behaviour that is being observed must be naturally occurring: the observations made must be non-intrusive and not change the behaviour of others in any way. In a commercial setting, an ethnographical study requires you as the researcher to become part of the community you are investigating and to participate in the usage of the product as well as in other forms of behaviours associated with the product or service.

Preparation

You are advised to locate published consumer research ethnographies and to read carefully through several of these articles. Reading good consumer ethnographies is an excellent way to learn how these types of studies are written up and the ways in which ethnographic research is conducted. We suggest that while doing so, you reflect upon your own research process and data analysis, which will help you develop an understanding of searching out themes and theories from your own research results.

You need to think about where and when you might encounter people using the product or service in focus and make plans to enable these encounters during the research period. Before going into an ethnographic data-gathering situation, you must attempt to concentrate upon two things:

1/ To keep in mind the research questions under investigation during the observation period
2/ To remain as unbiased as possible by not presupposing that a behaviour will or will not occur or to impose an interpretation about why a behaviour happens or does not happen

Location

Ethnographic observations are best carried out in places or situations in which the product or service at the centre of your research usually occurs. Consequently, you will have to think about the most effective environment in which to make your observations.

Materials

There are few materials involved in ethnographic procedures. As you do not want to draw attention to yourself when observing a crowd or an individual, no recording devices should be carried during the procedure. You may carry a notebook and/or a smart phone, etc., on which you will record your impressions and interpretations IMMEDIATELY AFTER an observation has been completed. Recordings should not be taken during the observation period or in the observation location.

Participants

Participants are not recruited for this procedure but constitute members of the public carrying out their daily activities.

Procedure

1/ You should discuss, as a team, where, when, and how you will be able to unobtrusively observe the usage of your product or service.
2/ You will then plan and prepare a schedule for making the observations
3/ During the procedure do not attract attention to yourself but simply observe what is happening around you.
4/ An observation should last 15 to 30 minutes.
5/ Immediately after completing an observation depart from the setting to document all significant details that you can remember, as well as your personal reactions to the observation period.

Results

The results that you will produce in your ethnographic procedures will take the form of comments and notations recorded immediately after the experience. The notes and reflections should also consider your role in the observation process and any errors you made with respect to being a neutral, undisclosed observer.

Analyses

Analyses performed upon the observational data will include the description of the actions of the subjects in the study. These actions should be documented as accurately as possible. Following the writing-up of the fieldwork observations and reflections, your research team should critically examine the context within which the observation was undertaken and the actions studied in an attempt to interpret the meaning of the data in relation to the research questions.

Chapter 18. Netnography

Outline

The aim of netnography is to uncover the culture of consumption and usage of online communities surrounding a product or service. As netnography entails research upon human subjects, a netnographic project within a university setting requires approval by the university's Institutional Review Board (IRB). A project that has been approved will then involve the researcher becoming immersed within a living online community. The format of this immersion will vary but usually requires the researcher to engage in debate with members of fora and other types of online communities that are specifically related to the product or service of interest.

However, as IRB approval is often a lengthy process and cannot always be achieved within the timeframe available for a course in netnography, IRB approval is not often sought. Therefore readers who are college students should not interact in online groups when conducting a netnography. **You should not join any fora, ask questions online, nor play an active role in such groups.** Rather, we suggest you scour the Internet to find appropriate fora to observe and attempt to make assessments of the online communities' relationship and reaction to the research product or service without posting to the group or in any other way taking part in the group.

Preparation

Preparation for netnographic procedures involves identifying appropriate online resources and deciding on when and where to undertake the netnography (more details are given below).

Location

You may perform the netnography wherever you are able to gain Internet access.

Materials

Online computer access and a means of taking notes about the search being conducted are the only materials required.

Participants

The participants in a netnography are members of the online community that is being viewed. As already stated, in a commercial setting the researcher would become an active member of the online community. Ethicality requires that an investigator declare his or her status and purpose to the list moderator of an online group and then again to the online group members after he or she has received permission from the moderator. Students who are undertaking a netnography as part of a research project that has not sought approval from an IRB, may only gather **publically available** postings. **In order not to compromise any of the posters of communication, the posters must not be identified in any way.**

Procedure

You will need to spend considerable time searching on the Internet for locations that contain discussions and other information about your product or service from a cultural perspective. This last point is important to emphasize: a netnography does not 'per se' collect online information or data about a product or service. Rather, the information that is of interest in a netnography is that which arises from online community exchanges. For example, discussion fora on the product or on similar products are of interest, as are user and customers' comments on commercial sites such as Amazon. There are an enormous number of potential sites that may yield information that assist you to locate a product or service within its online culture.

Results

When sampling publicly available postings, the results will take the form of verbatim comments made in fora, or in other online sites that present a discussion or user opinions about your product or service. Online user sites often include numerical data, for instance, the number of people supporting a user comment (the ubiquitous *like* button). This form of quantitative information may be included in your report but should not be a major component of your analysis, report, or presentation.

Analyses

What you are attempting to reveal in a netnography are the complex cultural understandings and usages of products and services, as well as, the insightful impacts of these revelations upon the product or service you are investigating. The fact that netnographies have the potential to produce rich information about your area of interest is one of the reasons for not concentrating upon simple, numerical data, such as the number of users agreeing with a particular statement. Themes and quotations are again the currency of netnographic analyses (thematic analysis is used in many approaches to qualitative research covered in this book and you are guided to the index to read details about this procedure at other locations).

Chapter 19. Visual Ethnography

Outline

We have all seen collections of photographs that are grouped together to tell a story. Often these collections constitute coffee table books or travel accounts. The visual ethnography that you can assemble will be very similar to one of these books but rather than being about a country, city, or journey, the collected photographs will relate to your investigation about a product or service. The assemblage may be conceived broadly and include images that are not of the product or service themselves, yet still provide information about the product's or service's cultural use and consumption.

Preparation

Prior to conducting this procedure you will need to select a large group of images from which you will then choose a few pictures for inclusion in your visual ethnography project. These photographs or images should be in the public domain. Freely available pictures, which are not copyrighted, can be found on the Internet from sites that do not require subscriptions. If you take your own photos, you must not use images of recognizable individuals. Researchers must ensure that no person is identifiable in any of the outputs of their research (faces, etc., must be blurred before inclusion in the report or presentation) and this anonymity extends to automobiles (license plates blurred prior to use) and to any other visual information from which someone may be identified.

Location

The visual ethnography can be developed on your computer.

Materials

See preparation section above.

Participants

You, or you and your team, may be the participants in this procedure.

Procedure

Your exploration for suitable visual ethnographic images should be guided by: 1/ a search/review of relevant literature; 2/ results from the research procedures you have already conducted. You may search online and real-world image banks and archives in order to identify appropriate photographs for the project. A limited number of photographs should be used, all of which conform to the limitations given in the preparation section above. You should also use their own knowledge of the product or service to find images with metaphorical meaning.

Results

The outcome of the visual ethnography project takes the form of a collection of five to ten digital images. These will be presented in the final visual ethnography with just enough text to unambiguously establish a metaphorical story about the topic under study.

Analyses

The final selection of images should be arranged to reflect the themes and/or metaphors that you are attempting to communicate about the product or service. Pictures may also be assembled in a manner that conveys a narrative regarding the research topic: for instance, client experiences, shopping experiences, relations with products, etc. You should not include images that duplicate messages alluded to by other photos already selected.

Chapter 20. Artefacts

Outline

The artefacts that you collect will be any physical items made by human beings that are associated with the product or service, such as packaging, advertising and promotion materials.

Preparation

You should brainstorm to think carefully about what sort of materials would help convey the cultural significance of the product or service you are investigating.

Location

Artefacts can be found in almost any situation or environment depending upon the topic of research interest.

Materials

There are no specific materials needed to conduct this approach to research. You should however clearly document the sources of the artefacts that you utilise for the project.

Participants

You, the investigator(s) will be the participant(s) and gather the artefact materials.

Procedure

You must identify possible sources for your choice of artefacts. Artefacts are then searched out from different locations and brought back for personal reflection or to the research team for discussion.

Results

After collecting the items, you must decide which artefacts best convey the central message of the investigation. These items should be retained and the others discarded. We suggest that you use a limited number of artefacts to illustrate your conclusions. Photographs of the artefacts can be included in the body of the research report if the images contribute significantly to communicating the meaning of the account or placed in the appendices if the images are of peripheral importance.

Analyses

You will carefully study the artefacts, both as individual objects and as a coherent group of items. You should write descriptions of your responses, which will include: aesthetic impressions of the objects, understandings of the usage and historical context of the items, and how the artefacts are relevant to the advertising of the product or service in focus. Next, you will seek out published research material that has already described a comparable artefact or set of artefacts. It is extremely useful if you familiarize yourself with how other researchers have interpreted and understood similar objects to those in their own study. How do these perceptions compare? How are they similar? How do they differ? Ask why this is. Finally, decide upon your interpretation and present your conclusions in relation to the other scholars' work. Put forward explanations for your interpretation, which may also include information from other primary research data.

The physical items that have been collected can perhaps best be thought of as support material to a larger research study. It is unlikely in a learning process such as a student project that the gathered artefacts will produce any surprises, however, these objects are useful as an effective compliment to the development of the analysis-based narrative of a research report.

Chapter 21. Archives

Outline

Archival data or materials take the form of printed documents, web-based/digital records, and other configurations of information. There is a thin line dividing archival materials from that found in secondary or literature research. Indeed, in this study guide no distinction will be explicitly made.

Preparation

Many kinds of databases exist which contain archival information. In order to prepare for archival inquiry, you must think broadly to identify sources (online and real-world) for particulars about your service or product.

Rather than simply hunting on Google or some other search engine about the product of interest, you should develop specific queries about your topic in an attempt to produce consequential information relevant to the guiding question(s) of the overall project. For example, if your research is looking at the release of a new model of a consumer product, then the history of that product's development may be of interest. In such a case, product history should be the basis of the search. Alternatively, if your research question involves bringing a product to a new geographical region then your search may include focusing upon the product, as it exists in other geographical regions.

The important thing to remember here is that the more focused your search, the more likely the information you discover will be of importance and relevant to your project.

Location

Many archival sources are available online and you will be able to conduct searches from home, college, etc. Other physical archives may be located in libraries, collections facilities, town halls, company headquarters, publishers, etc. If this type of archive is to be used, you need to visit these locations.

Materials

The materials involved in an archival search include computer access and some way of recording the gathered material.

Participants

No participants are involved in completing a research task in archival research. However, if physical archives are accessed, contact must be made with archivists, librarians, curators, etc.

Procedure

The archival search procedure first involves listing key words, phrases, and other linguistic terms pertinent to your topic. An example of these terms may assist to understand this process. Thus, a study looking at how college professors' have historically used literature and other published resources in their research and teaching, may include terms that relate to: the time/period (now; future, in the last 20 years; etc.); the materials (e.g., digital publications; magazines; books; journals; blogs…); what these materials are used for (e.g., used directly in teaching; background reading; assigned reading; generating research questions; providing background to a research project); where the materials are used (e.g., in the classroom; in a laboratory; at the student's home; in the professors' office; in the library, etc.); and other terms as are appropriate. These terms are then used to sift through databases to identify documents associated with your area of interest. Prior to commencing an archival search it is useful for your research team to have a clear strategy that specifies the particular archives to be examined and identifies the expected purpose for the newly acquired information. The material gathered must include the: database used; author of the archival item; title; where and when the item was published; page numbers; URL; DOI; etc.).

Results

The results in an archival research are the collected archival items in digital or printed format, or selected extracts taken from these items.

Analyses

Analysis will take the form of reading through archival texts and looking at archival images to identify features in these documents that provide information that is useful to your overall project. How you expect to use this information in your research project will guide both the material you have gathered and how you analyse and present the information from these searches. Analysis of archival materials may provide information about a community's historical, contemporary and geographic placement, as well as its financial and trading practices, along with other details about your research product or service.

Chapter 22. Journals and Diaries

Outline

Journal keeping is a practice in which people produce entries in a journal or diary, and explore their thoughts and feelings around experiences, or, in a consumer research class, around a product, service or concept. The notion behind this research approach is that consumers or diarists may reveal more about how they have been using a product or service along with their associated ideas, impressions, opinions, etc., within the comfort of their own homes or private space. Journaling can be practiced using books, notepads, digital equipment such as computers, still and video cameras, Smartphones, etc. In this guide, we suggest the participants reflect upon a product, service, or other topic and document these reflections in a specified way, at particular times, and over a certain amount of days.

Preparation

The preparation stage of journal keeping requires careful consideration. These choices include deciding: what format the journal will take (diary, video, blog, etc.); whether to include images with the text (remember some people do not enjoy writing); the frequency of entry to which participants will commit (from multiple times a day to weekly, etc.); whether entries will be responses to predetermined questions or be free text; whether responses will involve checking boxes, recording numbers, or writing text; over what period of time the diary will be kept, the length of each entry, etc. Many other questions will need to be answered prior to undertaking a journaling procedure.

Location

In some consumer research instances, the location for the journaling activities may be left up to the participant. However, dependent upon the type of product or service, the researchers may wish the participant to have the products close at hand, or to have completed a day's usage of the product or service (i.e., after retiring for the night, completing the diary task in bed), or to be actually using the product or service at the time of the journaling. These decisions may effect the setting in which participants are asked to complete their journals.

Materials

The veritable journals that participants are asked to keep will be of varied types. The type will be determined by answers to the questions that have been raised in the *preparation* and *location* sections above, as well as, to what the project research question(s) are asking in general and the journal procedure in particular. The journal itself will have to be prepared by members of the research team and given to participants. The journal may take many forms. For example it may be a traditional paper journal, a virtual diary emailed to participants or websites that participants must log into, etc. You must include a comprehensible and well-written introduction in all forms of journaling in order to guide participants unambiguously through the tasks that are required of them. Brief directions should be included at every location where participants make a journal entry. Full instructions must also be clearly positioned in the journal book, virtual diary, website, etc., so that participants can easily locate them if they have questions about completing a journal task.

Participants

If you are working as an individual then you may keep a journal on your own product or service in order to understand the procedure. If you are working in a team, you may want to ask another team member to keep a journal for you and offer to keep one for them.

Procedure

Journals should be kept for a period of 10 days (in commercial situations journals are usually kept over a longer portion of time). Participants will be presented with the journaling materials, including a journal in the chosen format and any other support or stimulus materials, such as information and instructions that the participant may need to read before diary completion. Researchers must explain to participants how and when they should return the diaries to the research team. Participants should be asked to take approximately 20 minutes a day to work on their diary entries.

Results

Journal results will take the form specified (text, images, video, etc.).

Analyses

Data that arises from journaling procedures can be analysed in many ways. Exactly how data will be analysed will be dependent upon the type of journaling that you or your team has chosen. A common form of journaling is when respondents are asked to keep an open text diary and to make an entry once a day. This format of data can be analysed as any other textual material. You will attempt to identify themes present in the data either through multiple readings of the journal transcripts or by using one of the many proprietary software packages that are available to specifically analyse qualitative textual data.

As with all narrative forms of data analysis, you are forewarned against simply counting the number of times a word, phrase, or sentiment appears in a transcript. Numerical information may provide a minimal amount of interest but invites methodological and philosophical problems when a researcher attempts to add or aggregate expressions from different participants. Moreover, analyses that simply identify the frequency of textual features miss out on the deeper meanings, such as what may be purported, intended or conveyed by a varied use of language.

Chapter 23. Autoethnography

Outline

Autoethnography is a process in which the researcher becomes the respondent and deliberately exposes him or herself to the product or service that is of interest and then records these observations as they relate to the product or service. Students may experience the autoethnographic process over a period of 7 to 14 days during which they will use a "fly on the wall" approach (self-observation) and not interact directly with other people.

Preparation

As the researcher is also the respondent in an autoethnography, there is always the very real possibility that the results arising from this type of study will be extremely biased. This is due to the fact that autoethnographers do not simply observe and record their observations in a detached manner, but rather they experience the product directly, as a customer would, and what they record is their own understanding of the product. Therefore, researchers must attempt the extremely difficult task of being unbiased. They must take all possible measures to keep an open mind and not let their beliefs, expectations, etc., colour their observations and interpretations of what they see and hear. Furthermore, before undertaking an autoethnography, you must clearly identify what and whom you will be observing and where and when you will be doing this.

Location

The autoethnography will be undertaken in settings that are relevant to your product, service or concept. You should carefully and thoroughly plan the locations, times, dates, etc.

Materials

You need to arrange how you will document your observations during the procedure. Notes must be taken in a book or on a tablet, etc. A phone may be used to capture images.

Participants

There are no participants in an autoethnography as you become your own research subject.

Procedure

You will have already identified where and when you are to make your observations and you should plan to undertake these observations over a period of 7 to 14 days. It is important to be unobtrusive when the observer is conducting research. Taking notes or other forms of documentation whilst in the field site should be avoided, as this is disruptive to your observation procedure and may draw attention to you as a researcher. After remaining inconspicuous at the observation site for 15–30 minutes, you may leave the location to document thoughts and feelings about the experience.

Results

The data that you collect will take the form of recollections of your own experiences and your reflections upon these. You may also want to assemble other texts and images and if applicable gather artefactual materials.

Analyses

Autoethnographies are analysed to reveal themes that are pertinent to the research question(s). Particular care must be taken when attempting to analyse the data that arises from autoethnographic procedures as the data has been produced by the researcher. **This being the case, it is important that another researcher, or other team members, perform the analyses to help mediate the extent of researcher/participant bias.**

Section 4 – Writing and Analysing a Research Report

Chapter 24. The Structure of an Academic Article/Report

If you have actively followed our suggestions for implementing the ten approaches to qualitative consumer research, you will have noticed that these procedures produce a large body of information. The question then arises of what you should do with all the data, concepts and ideas. In order to make sense of the research, the results from each procedure will need to be structured and combined to produce insights that are easily discernable and useful to others, e.g. your employer or client. This structured presentation will take the form of either, or both, an oral account or a written academic report.

However, the importance of learning how to write an academic report extends far beyond the purpose of presenting your findings. As a student and in your later professional life, you will read, present, write, and critically evaluate your own work as well as review and write about other reported research. The following description intends to familiarise you with the structure of a research article/report so that you may better understand and analyse published material and develop the skills to organize and present your own research project.

Research articles have a format that is designed to clearly communicate the process and findings of a research project. The scientific report is traditionally divided into six sections and the following expatiation will follow this format. It should be noted that the template that is presented here is the 'most typical' design for a scientific or structured report. However, each piece of research that is conducted will have its own inherent design: a design that may cause the typical structure to be adapted or modified to better present information in a clear and unambiguous manner. This checklist will also help you in classes when you are asked to read, review, or critique an article or other form of publication by offering you a framework for your appraisal. Furthermore, learning to critically review official and research report writing will assist you to develop a model for your own write-up, e.g. of the team research project.

Below are the six sections of the report/article and their typical content.

The Research Paper

A/ Abstract/summary/executive summary
B/ Introduction
C/ Methods
D/ Results
E/ Discussion
F/ References

A. Abstract/summary/executive summary

The list above is a summary of the structure that successfully communicates the contents of a piece of research in which the purpose, scope, and major findings of the research/article content are presented.

It is common practice for people to only read the title and abstract of an article or report. From perusal of the abstract, readers determine whether they will continue reading the article. Therefore, it is very important that the abstract is clearly and concisely written and conveys the following information: what was done in the research; the main results of the research; and the main conclusions of the research. When evaluating the summary a student should ask the following questions:

Questions to ask about the abstract

1/ Is the abstract intelligible?
2/ Does the abstract reproduce and accurately describe the objectives and results of the paper/research?
3/ Does the abstract include data not presented in the paper?
4/ Does the abstract include material or make claims that cannot be substantiated by the results/data?

B. Introduction

In the introduction the author needs to present a logically structured background to the research that follows. The introduction to a research article is a little like the introduction to a story in that it needs to contain all of the relevant background information in order that later sections of the writing may be read and easily understood. In the case of a research report, the introduction must include a review of the existing literature and other information that is directly pertinent to the study. By the time the reader has completed reading the introductory section, she or he should understand the background to the research and believe (through the author's guiding words) that there is only one possible course of action open to the researchers, which is to conduct the study that they conducted and in the manner in which they conducted it. In order to achieve this aim, you must present the background information to the research and provide a clear context for the study. Many investigations begin by identifying a correlation or association in the research literature from empirical observations or observing patterns in data: details of these observations should be included in the introduction as they apply to your project.

At the conclusion of the introduction section you must explicitly state your research question or scientifically derived hypothesis. For instance: the research question and why this research is important. In this brief section any competing hypotheses or theories may be mentioned.

Questions that you may ask about the introduction include:

1/ What reasons are given to undertake the study?
2/ Is the background to the research clearly presented?
3/ Is enough background information presented to allow the reader to understand the aims and objectives of the study?

C. Methods

Next comes the methods section, which describes clearly, succinctly, and chronologically what was done and how this was done. When planning or evaluating the methods section you should be able to answer, "yes" to the following general question:

"Could someone else repeat this research with the information that has been provided?"

If the answer to the above question is "no," then the methods section is incomplete. In order to thoroughly review the methods section, ask the following questions:

1/ Were the research methods described in enough detail to allow other researchers to repeat or extend the study?
2/ Were adequate references cited to allow a clear understanding of the methods used (unfortunately, citations about the methods used in a piece of research are often omitted from citation lists)?
3/ Did the researcher clearly and carefully report how the investigators modified any of the methodologies employed and in enough detail to allow other researchers to use the modified approaches?
4/ When describing their methods, did the authors make it clear why they chose to use those particular procedures?
5/ Did the authors list any problems, potential problems, or limitations of the chosen methodology?
6/ If descriptive statistical procedures (graphs, frequency representations, etc.) were used, were they thoroughly described?
7/ Were the descriptive statistical methods appropriate for the study, type of data, and research questions?

D. Results

The results section in an article presents the key findings and non-findings from a research project. In qualitative research, trends in the data are high-

133

lighted in a concise and easily understandable manner. This often takes the form of themes that emerge from the data such as patterns of respondent characteristics, and/or patterns of product, service, concept, or background characteristics. Questions to ask about the results:

1/ Do the results presented appropriately address the stated objectives of the research?

2/ Do the results presented make sense: make sense both as written prose and in terms of the background to the project that was put forth in the report's introductory section?

3/ Are tables and figures appropriately used and labelled, so that the data they contain may be clearly understood?

4/ Are the analyses used appropriate for the data, research questions, and hypotheses?

E. Discussion

In the discussion the background to the research, as presented in the report's introduction, is blended with the results of the investigation. The question(s) and/or hypothesis presented at the end of the introduction section are evaluated in reference to the newly discovered results. This section should unify the story that the research is attempting to tell. This section should not be a repetition of the results but should synthesize the information in the manner suggested above. In the discussion section the authors should evaluate potential and/or probable explanations for the results they obtained. Differences and similarities that have been discovered between the present research and comparable past research studies should be noted and attempts should be made to explain these similarities or discrepancies.

When reading an article, it is important to be aware of the authors' assertions and if they have gone beyond the information presented in their research findings or if they are making claims that stretch the results. It is also important to consider whether the researcher has attempted to generalize beyond the reasonable bounds of the procedures and sample used. Finally, new literature should not be introduced in the discussion as any research findings cited in the study should have been introduced earlier in the introduction section of the report.

Questions to ask about the discussion:

1/ Were the stated objectives of the research project met? If not, have the researchers provided adequate reasons for failing to meet these objectives?

2/ Do the authors discuss the results of the present study in relation to similar studies, and is the scope of similar studies adequate?

3/ Do the authors indulge in needless speculation?

4/ Do the results that are presented possess ecological validity (are they important within a real world context)?

5/ Are the limitations of the study/data clearly interpreted, discussed, and understood by the authors?

F. References

Although comments about cited references have already been made, some additional questions will recapitulate and expand upon these observations:

Questions to be asked about the references/citations

1/ Do the references cited allow the authors to make the claims they make?

2/ Do authors cite their own publications needlessly?

3/ Are the sources cited recent enough to allow the research to be up to date with current knowledge?

4/ Are older important sources cited that allow the research to be well grounded in relevant theory?

5/ Are the references provided in a consistent and recognized citation format?

General questions about the paper

1/ What is/are the central/vital message(s) in the article?

2/ Is there a "so what" factor associated with the research?

It is therefore apparent that in both planning and writing your own academic report, as well as in evaluating another researcher's work, you essentially use the same steps. Ideally, when writing your own text, you will use the above suggestions while composing the report and then go through the manuscript again, attempting to analyse and improve it according to the criteria we presented. Therefore, these criteria both provide you with a template to thoroughly understand another researcher's work – and to write a concise, informative report about your own research.

General Writing Tips & Suggestions

There are several suggestions that are in essence "good practice" when writing a research report. These include the following:

1/ Before writing-up the report, you should produce a clear outline of the research project, using the above suggested sections and incorporate particular content that relates to the study

2/ When you first use a term that has either a specific or ambiguous meaning, provide an explicit definition of how this term is employed in your report

3/ Write accurately, concisely, and to the point

4/ Make sure your paper follows a logical sequence and moves smoothly from one section to the next

5/ Avoid writing in a passive voice as this is often confusing for readers

6/ Ask other people to read your written work (if possible, a- someone knowledgeable about the topic of your research, b- someone who meets the criteria for inclusion in your sample but has not been involved in any way in the research, c- a lay person (i.e., a relative, friend). It is often intimidating to have other people read your work but this may well make the report a stronger and more under-standable document.

7/ Plan to finish the report early so that you have a few days to return to it and do final edits before submission of the final document. A fresh outlook will help you identify poor structure, incorrect grammar, improper phrasing, etc.

8/ Do a final proofread and spelling check

Appendices

Appendix A. Outline for a Course in Qualitative Research Methods in Consumer Psychology

We don't expect our readers, to become experts in qualitative research methods just by reading this study guide. In fact, the text merely provides the basics of the ten research methods presented. We recommend you read this publication in conjunction with a more comprehensive textbook and/or attend a practical program of study on the topic. In what follows, we explain the outline of a course that the first author teaches. Readers who are lecturers may use this outline as a template for designing their own courses; student readers may browse through it in order to get an idea of how such a course complements the procedures discussed in this guide.

Four Assessed Core Elements

It may be useful for readers to think of this introductory course in qualitative research methods to consist of four main integrated core elements, each of which will be assessed. The four elements are specified in figure 7. Students must attend all classes and take an active part in discussions and other specified activities. Students are required to complete all assigned readings. In addition, each student is responsible for finding, reviewing, and presenting two published research articles from refereed journals (including a hypothetical research design), and finally, as a member of a research team, each student shares in the production and completion of a bona fide research project.

One of the aims of this course is to enhance students' critical reading skills in order that they are able to accurately analyse a wide variety of documents. Students and professionals will encounter many different formats of articles, reports and publications that in some way can be seen as being 'official' in nature. What is meant by *official documents* is that official publications purport to convey factual information or to present an authoritative opinion and are not primarily advertising or promotional material. Whilst all documents, to some extent, carry a slant on the truth, these official articles, reports, files etc., will be evaluated by students in terms of their clarity of argument and lack of bias. The course emphasizes reading these official types of publications: how to scrutinize, and to some extent, how to produce this format of document (see Section 4). At this point it is useful to note that official articles are usually the product of research. As this is the case, the structure of the research process itself will impact the structure of research writing: the research process provides a rationale for the structure of the written report/article.

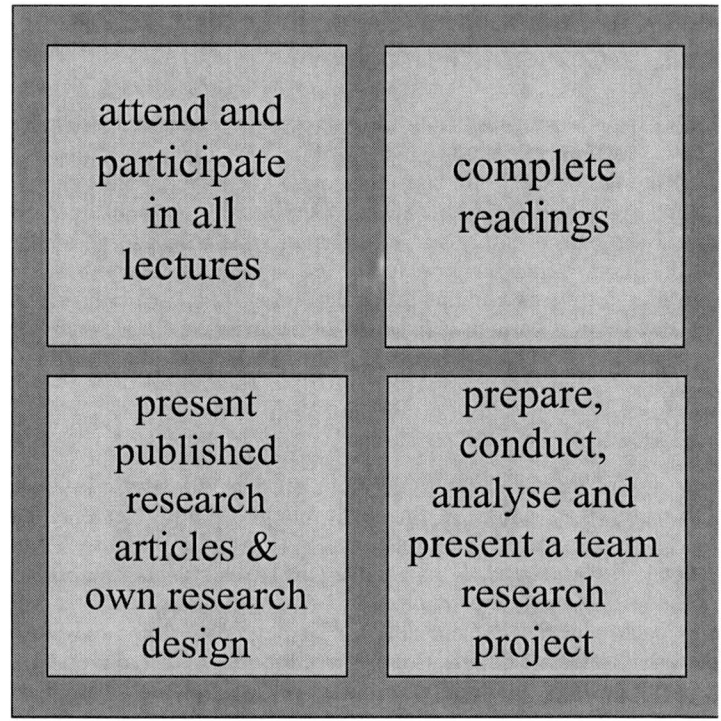

Figure 7. Four Core Elements

Through sharing oral presentations students learn about the strengths and weaknesses of the rich information provided by ethnography and other non-sampling based research approaches and how to employ these texts as a basis from which to design their own research project. Each student becomes a member of a group that designs a research project that yields ethnographic insight, an understanding of consumer psychology and cultural analysis of the service or product of interest. Through the readings and in-class discussions, students examine consumers' wants, needs, and likes, and how these influence article and service usage, evaluation, purchase and marketing. These group projects encourage appreciation of the validity and usefulness of qualitative research procedures through a series of data gathering and analysis enterprises. Procedures will be selected from: ethnography/netnography, artefact based study, mind mapping, sort techniques, journaling/blogs/Smartphone journals, creativity sessions, sponsored shopping, in-depth-interviews (IDI), and focus group interviews (FGI). Understanding and applying these procedures helps students to develop the skills to build up a tool kit of qualitative research methods in order to better respond to the applied questions of marketers. Students learn to write a report crafted to answer clients' questions, and as a research team, how to orally present this account to an audience. Finally, through team and individual work, students will be provided with the opportunity to realize the beneficial insights gained from understanding how customers actually use, choose, and engage with products and services.

Summary

Upon completion of the activities outlined in this course, each student will have attained several research skills and increased their understanding of the qualitative research process within the area of consumer psychology. Below are the more specific outcomes for this type of course.

Students will:

1/ Have developed an understanding of the range of qualitative research methods used in marketing research
2/ Have gained understanding of different types of qualitative research methods and when it is appropriate to use each of these
3/ Have had experience using basic qualitative research skills
4/ Be able to understand and evaluate published qualitative research studies
5/ Be able to understand the ethical principles associated with conducting trustworthy and valid qualitative research with human participants
6/ Have the ability to recognize and respond appropriately to ethical issues associated with this type of research
7/ Have designed and developed a qualitative research project that demonstrates an awareness of the factors that are associated with qualitative research design
8/ Have had practice communicating the results of your research project
9/ Have selected, critiqued and presented a published qualitative consumer psychology research article

This course is comprised of four interrelated tasks, all of which have been specifically designed to understand and apply the knowledge content of the previous three sections of the study guide, however, modifications and changes by other instructors will be expected. The specific tasks associated with this course model are listed below.

1/   Research Articles Evaluation and Hypothetical Research Design Presentation

2/   Vignette (see details later in this appendix)

3/   Team Research Project, including Written Report and Team Oral Presentation

4/   Individual Poster Presentation

Throughout the semester, students will be expected to vigorously seek out library resources (physically and online), search databases, and undertake the specified writing associated with their research project. All written work should be in APA format or in some other widely used citation and writing style such as Harvard, etc. (see reading list for details of the APA style handbook). Students are asked to keep a copy of all materials submitted. In each piece of written work associated with this course and with all data acquired from any kind of research project, students must respect the confidentiality of every participant. Students and their research teams must also make arrangements to secure the data that arises from their research projects.

In the following subsections, details for an introductory course in consumer psychology are presented.

1/ Evaluation of Research Articles and Hypothetical Research Design Presentation

It is recommended that all students during the semester make a presentation, which commences with a critique of two research articles and concludes with the student's own hypothetical design for a research study. During most class periods throughout the semester, two selected students will be required to present their review of two published qualitative research articles and to conclude their presentation with their own design for investigating a product, service, or concept (not the ones in the articles). By designing a new study and applying the procedures described in either or both of the articles reviewed, students will demonstrate their understanding of the methods critiqued. We will now discuss this presentation in two parts: A/ Evaluation of Research Articles, B/ Hypothetical Research Design Component of Articles Presentation.

A/ Evaluation of Research Articles

The article reviews will take the following format: one article will be presented and then a second article will be contrasted with the first in terms of subject matter, procedures, analyses techniques, etc. The student will **not** actually undertake the research for the design segment, but merely develop a framework to employ the specific procedures used in the articles to a different product, etc., and to propose the types of results that might be expected

With guidance from their professor students will locate and then choose their own qualitative research articles to review. The articles students select need to contain extensive details of the qualitative research methodology used in the research. The choice of articles should relate to a student's particular interests and this association should be demonstrated in the presentation. Details must be provided during the presentation of how and where the articles were found (databases used, key words/terms employed by the student). The chosen articles should focus upon issues within marketing or allied subjects (broadly construed, e.g., psychology, distribution, etc.). However, the presentation's emphasis must be the student's own critique of the qualitative research methods and qualitative analysis techniques used in the accounts.

These presentations should include PowerPoint (or equivalent) and are to last approximately 15 minutes with up to five more minutes for questions from colleagues. Peer support and interaction are important components of the article presentation. Students are expected to actively participate in a critique of each other's talks. These criticisms of student presentations require clear vision, honesty and sensitivity.

Each student must apply the following structure to his or her presentation. The order in which the elements are listed below forms a template for a logical talk[10]. Students may include sections other than those listed below.

Each presentation must incorporate the following information for both of the two research articles:

1/ Articles titles, names and affiliations of author(s)
2/ Where the articles were published (which journals)
3/ The year the articles were published
4/ How and where students found the articles
5/ A brief summary of the research findings that are presented in the two articles
6/ Specifics of the qualitative methodologies used in the research
7/ Details of the results of the two pieces of research
8/ Your critique of the methods used and of the articles in general
9/ Provide particulars of any other types of research methods (concentrating upon qualitative methods) that could have been used and what students expect each of these approaches would have contributed to the research
9/ Why students think these two studies are relevant to marketing research/consumer psychology research
10/ Any implications for future research

---

10   This structure should also be used to design your final written report.

The two articles that students select may be presented consecutively or in parallel. Whichever way they choose to present the articles, contrasts between the studies must be examined. The procedures should be discussed knowledgably within the hypothetical research design you present as a conclusion.

Students' grades for the article presentation will be based on the analyses they present under the compulsory content headings given above and their engagement with the rest of the class in a relevant discussion. If students are not presenting an article, they are still expected to attend all presentations made by other students, and to take an active part in these events by asking applicable questions. Furthermore, they are not to use email, the Internet, phones, etc., during another student's presentation as this is both rude and distracting to the student who is talking.

B/ Hypothetical Research Design Component of Articles Presentation

The final part of the presentation involves the design of a hypothetical research project. Students should take some or all of the research methods from the two papers they have presented and design a research project around a product or service using these methodologies. The product or service should **NOT** be included in either of the two articles they presented nor should the product or service they are evaluating be the same as their team research product.

In this section of students' presentation they **MUST INCLUDE** details about the following aspects of their hypothetical study:

1/ The product or service that is the focus of their research
2/ Their research question
3/ Who they would choose to be their sample and why
4/ The type of results that their research would be expected to produce
5/ How they would usefully employ these results in relation to their product or service

DO NOT ACTUALLY conduct the research project OR COLLECT ANY DATA.

For this presentation the student does NOT hand anything in to the faculty as all assessment is based upon the student's performance during the presentation.

2/ Vignette Project

This is a relatively short mid-semester assessment and will take the format of a team vignette.

A vignette may be defined as: *a brief account or description that brings forth strong emotions.* Vignettes can be thought of in several different ways. For example, in theatre, vignettes can be short scenes that produce a generalized impression of a moment or instance. Vignettes can also be acted scenes that provide sharp and insightful notions about a certain idea, character, or setting within a play. A vignette can be perceived as standing for something larger than itself and may take the form of short sketches.

Within the context of this class, a vignette is understood as a relatively short (approximately 20 minutes) skit or sketch that students write and perform. The contents of the vignette can be humorous, dramatic, documentary, etc., but must contain ALL of the topics that have been covered in the course up to and including the class immediately prior to the vignette assessment class. For example, in the sample class schedule given in Appendix C, the contents of vignettes should include all subjects covered in lectures 1 to 6. That is to say: What makes a good project; The research cycle; Practical research considerations; Ethics; Research methods, philosophies and approaches; Establishing clear research objectives; Mapping sentences; Research writing & reading; Project planning, design, recruitment; Sort approaches. This content forms the framework for the vignettes and should be elaborated upon by using additional topics discussed in class and material from students' research projects and outside reading.

As the vignette is a concept and a procedure that many students may not have previously encountered, vignettes can be discussed in class to dispel any misunderstandings. The vignettes are to summarise the subject matter of the course prior to the assessment class. The purpose of this evaluation is to gauge student progress on the material covered and to provide information about student learning to date. The vignette is an active procedure in which students review and affirm course content by applying their knowledge of qualitative methods in consumer psychology within a simulated real world context.

Students may design a vignette that takes the form of a research project, a TV show, a play, a family outing, a sports game, or any other of a thousand possibilities. However, the vignette **MUST NOT take the form of a game show (as this tends to demonstrate superficial understanding of qualitative research)**. Creativity is rewarded in this assessment; however, accuracy and thoroughness in the presentation of the course material are of primary importance and form the major components for grading.

All students in a team must take an active role in the development of the vignette and must participate equally in the vignette's performance.

3/ Team Research Project

Introduction

At the onset of the semester each student in this class will join with other classmates to form a research team. Each of these teams will identify a service, product, or concept suitable for investigation using qualitative research methods explored in this course. It is important to note that the product, service, or concept must be suitable for investigation by a series of different in-class research procedures (focus groups, in-depth interviews, netnographies, etc.) over the period of a single semester.

Team membership

Students will join together into groups of five to six persons. Students will select their own teams. Students should join groups because they feel comfortable working with the members of that team and because the service, product, or concept chosen is of interest to them. Sometimes after a topic has been selected a student may no longer wish to be a member of the team. All possible attempts will be made to relocate this student to a different group.

Research topic

Choosing the correct service, product or concept for your research is of vital importance to the successful completion of the project. Therefore, teams will discuss amongst themselves which service, product, or concept is of mutual interest to all team members. When choosing a service, product or concept for research, it is important to ask the following two questions:

1/ Is the service, product, or concept a suitable topic of study if class members comprise the respondent group?
2/ Is the service, product, or concept researchable through the approaches?

Examples of suitable products or services include: online companies such as Amazon, Uber, etc.; physically located bodies such as the regional transport authority; conceptual entities such as regional music festivals. Unsuitable projects may include: online, physically located or service firms from another country or region of which students have little or no experience; retirement homes, as students will have little or no experience of these; companies with little or no online presence. Furthermore, do not choose too broad a topic, such as the Olympic games, house sales, the news media, etc., as these may be difficult to investigate in a brief study such as this.

Major Components of the Project

Below is a summary timetable of the major events in the students' team research project. Many details of the project have been omitted from this schedule for the sake of clarity. **This is a general guideline. However, in the actual course students would find a definitive timetable attached to their syllabus to schedule their project.**

Weekproject work due

1-2	decide on research project; establish research team membership
3	present project proposal
3-10	conduct research
10-12	synthesise findings and write report
13	submit final report

Table 3: Research Procedures in this Course

Research Type	Questions to Ask
netnography	Are there readily accessible online consumer or user communities that are associated with your service, product or concept?
ethnography	Is your service, product, or concept readily observable in daily life (this means observable by you) in a situation, which does NOT require you to intervene with other people's actions or ask them questions?
visual ethnography	Are visual images available in the public domain (which are not subject to copyright restrictions) of your service, product, or concept? Are you easily able to take photographs of your service, product, or concept in a non-intrusive manner?
focus group interview	Is your service, product, or concept one that can be sensibly discussed by your class members? Do class members have direct experience and knowledge about your service, product, or concept (class members should not have to imagine your product or service)?
in-depth interview	(Ask the same questions as per the focus group) Will your fellow class members be able to talk in depth for 20 – 30 minutes about your service, product, or concept?
archival research	Are there historical documents (historical in this context means any pre-existing documentation) about your service, product, or concept that may be easily found in an online collection, database, library, etc.? Will you or other team members be able to gain access to this information during the timeframe of this course?
projective techniques	What are the subconscious motives that may underlie consumers' choices and other consumption related behaviours? How do you think suspected subconscious motives may best be accessed through existing projective techniques (i.e.,

	sorting items, mapping, free-writing, word association, per-sonification, etc.) and how may you design a projective research procedure to do this?
Artefact	Are there existing 'things' that you will be able to collect, photograph and display to represent how your product, service, or concept is used or understood within a cultural context? In this research 'things' are taken to mean objects that are related to, or used with your service, product, or concept such as packaging or promotional material. Can you employ artefacts to demonstrate the cultural signifi-cance of your service, product, or concept and possibly how this has changed over time or between locations?
Journals	Will your fellow class members be able to keep a diary or journal about their regular, preferably non-contrived, en-counters with your service, product, or concept? Will your classmates' comments be able to reflect their own opinions about your service, product, or concept (this is preferred) or must they imagine that they are a user of the service, product, or concept (not-preferred)?
autoethnography	Will you, as a researcher, be able to expose yourself to the service, product, or concept and then keep a diary about the experience? Will you be able to expose yourself to the service, product, or concept in a non-contrived or deliberate manner and will you be able to use the service, product, or concept in a way that is similar to how real world users would encounter your service, product or concept?

Project Proposal and Secondary Research

After students have finalized the choice of the service, product, or concept for their team project, each team must write a project proposal. The proposals are to be approximately one – two pages long, in Times New Roman, 12 point, and double-spaced. The contents of the proposal should follow a commonly used style of research proposal. The project proposal should include the fol-lowing subject matter:

research background	give details about your service, product, or concept and how this is used or encountered by the market segment you are investigating (in this research the segment is students from your college)
how your team will investi-gate the service, product or concept	list each of the above mentioned research approaches and suggest the type of information you expect each approach to reveal
how long the project will take	provide a timescale/timeline for your project

In the proposal, students will need to provide secondary information. Sec-ondary information is information that exists prior to the commencement of their research (for instance, existing articles, books, company reports, etc.).

Secondary information/research always exists for each project and must be provided. They should supply references (where they found the information) for the background to their project and cite sources consistently throughout using a standardized citation style (e.g., APA, Harvard, etc.). The secondary research they provide must clearly support the reasons for conducting their investigation and the limits of their inquiries. Research projects that are easier to manage generally arise from a proposal that provides a thorough research design based upon in-depth and extensive secondary information that describe the product/service and its current market.

Once again, recall that this is an in-class project and that most of students' primary data will be gathered within class during class hours. Other background information (e.g., financial models – return on investment, etc.) is not the emphasis of this research and should only be used to support your primary data. It will be assumed that college students are a viable market for the service, concept, or product you have selected. The research students conduct will then assess consumer opinion towards the existing product/service/concept, or some derivative of this, as this exists in reference to the particular college student market. If students wish, their product, service, or concept may be a new derivative of a product that already exists in that institution. Each research project will, to some extent, be unique. In the proposal students will provide the objectives of their research. Depending on the nature of the chosen product, service, or concept, and the secondary research relating to this, students' research *may* include the following objectives:

1/ To identify the target segments at the college for the product, service, or concept of interest
2/ To gather information that will provide suggestions regarding ways to tailor the product, service, or concept for commercial or public relation reasons
3/ To make suggestions about the positioning of the product, service, or concept within the college student market by considering consumer benefits, motivations, etc.
4/ To investigate the acceptability of the product, service or concept
5/ To make suggestions about the development of the brand image

Primary Research

Primary research is any research undertaken specifically to investigate a research problem. During the research students conduct for this course, they will carry out the following types of primary research projects: netnography; ethnography; visual ethnography; focus group interview; in-depth interview; archival research; projective techniques; artefact; journals and diaries; autoethnography.

Reporting Results

Each group will analyse their data using the qualitative analyses that are mentioned in the corresponding sections of this text[11]. As well as the qualitative analyses, each group may analyse their data (when this is appropriate) using descriptive statistics such as frequency, cross-tabs, measures of central tendency and dispersion and may display this data using appropriate graphs, etc. Each group will prepare an interim report and summary tables, which show the key findings from their studies (this is also called a top-line report).

Final Report

Length, letter size, and spacing

Each research group will submit one digital report and deliver one group presentation of the research findings. The final research report will be approximately thirty pages in length. This length is not including the references and appendices but contains all other sections of the document. The report should be typed in 12 point Times New Roman, double-spaced, and with standard margins all around. The final document should NOT be a hard copy but in **digital** form only.

Suggested structure of the report

The precise structure of the final report will be determined by the nature and scope of the team's research project. However, below is a generic template or what may be considered a brief outline for a "typical" project. This template shows the types of sections that are needed in the report and the team may decide to use these suggestions verbatim. However, when appropriate, a team may decide that the sections need minor adaptations or re-naming. The order of sections should always follow that shown in this study guide as this ordering provides a sensible story-like progression from developing the project to interpreting the results found. The numbers of pages that are suggested for each of the sections of the report are approximate and are only meant as a rough guide.

Structural template for the final report

In Figure 8 is a suggested structure for the write-up and presentation of the project report.

---

11   Interested readers may find further details in chapters 1, 4, 20, 21, in Qualitative Research Methods in Consumer Psychology: Ethnography and Culture.

Title, authors' names, affiliations, date, location

Acknowledgements/thanks
Summary/abstract
Introduction
Literature review/secondary research
Research objectives
Research methods
- Samples
- Materials
- Procedures
- Projective Techniques
- Focus Groups
- In-Depth Interviews
- Ethnography
- Netnography
- Visual Ethnography
- Artefact
- Archives
- Journals
- Autoethnography

Results/Findings
- Projective Techniques
- Focus Groups
- In-Depth Interviews
- Ethnography
- Netnography
- Visual Ethnography
- Artefact
- Archives
- Journals
- Autoethnography

Discussion/Conclusions
References/Bibliography/Reading List
Appendices

Figure 8. Structure of Final Report

Below students will find the sections of the report as specified in figure 8 along with further details for each of these components of the report (refer to Section 4 for a detailed account of how to write an academic report).

Title, authors' names, affiliations, date. Location

The front page of students' research reports should contain the following information:

- Title of the project
- Full names of all team members/authors
- Name of the educational institution
- Professor's name and the name of his or her department
- Date of the project
- Name and level of the course

Acknowledgements/thanks

This section may alternately be positioned at the end of the report and should include an acknowledgement and/or give thanks for assistance for conceptual or practical assistance during the research process and the writing of the report. This includes any support or encouragement that students have received (including family and friends if they consider the support they have given has been significant to the undertaking and completion of the project). All participants should be thanked.

The acknowledgements should be on a separate page(s).

Summary/abstract

The summary at the start of the research write-up is also called an executive summary or an abstract. This briefly presents the topic/area of the research project with a concise outline of the main or most pertinent research findings. References or citations, graphs, illustrations, etc., do not appear in the summary. The summary may be the only part of the report that people read. Therefore, the summary must concisely embody all findings. The summary ought to have enough detail to allow readers to determine whether or not they want to look at the rest of the report. However, the summary should not attempt to explicitly 'sell' the report but simply inform readers about the report's content, the reason why the study was undertaken, the most important results, the conclusions, and how these conclusions relate to the research questions.

The summary should be one separate page in length (maximum).

Introduction

The introduction presents the topic of research (the product, service or concept that students will be investigating) to the reader. Pertinent aspects relating to the background of the research are to be noted in this introduction. For example: a brief statement of why the research is being undertaken and why the researchers find this product, service or concept, of interest.

The introduction should be approximately one or two pages in length.

Literature review/secondary research

In this section students will elaborate upon the introductory section by including details such as a: situation analysis, market analysis, marketing problems, etc. A SWOT (strengths, weaknesses, opportunities, tactics) report may be prepared if the team feels that readers will better understand the reasons for the research after they have read a SWOT analysis. Other relevant background materials collected from newspapers, magazines, book chapters, blogs, websites, etc. should be included in this section. Examples may include particulars about a company, products, services, concepts or brands as well as about competing products, services, companies, etc. Students should include information that helps readers to better understand the products, service, etc., and the reason for undertaking this research project. Students should use the secondary research information to build a case for conducting their research project.

The literature review should be approximately five to seven pages in length including the SWOT analysis.

Research objectives

The research objectives follow the literature review, as the literature review is written to support the reasons for which teams are conducting the research. Once the reader has read the introduction and then the literature review, he or she should be in no doubt that a piece of research needs to be conducted to 'fill' a gap in our understanding. The research objectives clearly detail the investigation to follow and how the study relates to the gap in knowledge the team is attempting to fill and to the understanding that the research is attempting to create.

This section should be a maximum of one page in length.

Research methods

In this section students must report on all the methodologies **used in their research** project. These will be the following approaches:

- Projective techniques
- Focus groups

- In-depth interviews
- Ethnography
- Netnography
- Visual ethnography
- Artefact
- Archives
- Journals
- Autoethnography

This component of the report is written up in the past tense with an active first person (plural: we; or singular: I) voice to explain what actually happened when each of the research procedures was conducted. This includes events that were unplanned or did not occur as researchers wished them to. The idea is to provide readers of the report with insight into what actually took place during the research rather than what the researcher planned to happen or wished to have happened. It is good to give details about what was planned and what actually occurred. Explanations of differences between students' planned procedure and what actually took place during their research should not be included at this stage of the research report but should be incorporated later on into the report's discussion and/or conclusion sections: It is in the discussion or conclusion section that the investigators consider the possible consequences of the procedural discrepancies and their impact on the overall project results.

In the method's section of the report students provide details under the following headings:

Samples

A sample may be described here as a defined subset taken from a clearly specified population of interest. This heading includes particulars of the samples used for all of the individual procedures of the overall research project (i.e., details such as: age, gender, year of study at college, college major, and any other characteristics that students think are pertinent to the product, service or concept they are studying for the project). For example, if they are studying a brand that is common on the West Coast of America but not on the East Coast, then including where students are from may be important. However, in this example it may be more useful to record whether the participant had familiarity with the product rather than assuming that coming from a location where the product exists equates familiarity with the brand.

Materials

Under this heading students must supply the full specification of all materials used in each of the individual research procedures, such as stimulus materials, pamphlets, brochures, computer-based materials, etc. If examples of a product are shown or if participants are asked to test the product, for instance, a beverage in a taste test, then full details about this procedure must be indicated including the amounts of the product given, where, when, and how this was given, etc.

Procedures

Here students should provide full details of all of the procedures that they conducted in the overall research project. This includes brief particulars of any instructions that were given to participants (note: copies of the actual instructions given, explanatory materials, etc., should be included in the appendices).

This section will be approximately four to seven pages long.

Results/Findings

The findings section is the true heart of the report. As with the previous sections, results should be presented in the following order of sub-sections.

- Projective techniques
- Focus groups
- In-depth interviews
- Ethnography
- Netnography
- Visual ethnography
- Artefact
- Archives
- Journals
- Autoethnography

In this results section students should draw attention to the important findings of their research. The results should be presented in a terse and succinct manner. They should not go into lengthy explanations regarding their results in this section. In the results section they should not relate their findings to the research objectives/hypotheses: again, this is done in the discussion section of the report. Results should be summarised in this section. What this means, for example, is that from the focus group or other interview-based research procedures, students may quote one or two verbatim comments to exemplify the overall findings of the strategy. Along with these examples they make overall summaries of what was said. Full details of the focus group, or other interviews, should be transcribed and presented in the appendices section of the report.

An example of an interview procedure is given above, but the same holds true for all of the procedures on which students report. For example, with a mapping procedure, the maps should be summarised in this section and all maps included in the appendices. In the journals procedure, findings should be summarised and one or two verbatim comments may be provided to evoke the atmosphere or feeling of the responses. The full journals/diaries should be included in the appendices.

The results section should be approximately three pages in length.

Discussion/Conclusions

The discussion and the conclusions must be written to explicitly address the research questions students stated in the research objectives section of the report. The Discussion/Conclusions section may be presented in one of two formats: - 1/ as two separate sections – 1- Discussion 2- Conclusions or - 2/ as one section – Discussion, with a distinct sub-section at the end of the section called Conclusions. In either instance, in the discussion section, students compare the actual results to the hypotheses and explain why they match or don't match. Part of why the results do not meet the expectations is explaining what went wrong and how the results might look different had everything gone right. The conclusion-section, then, offers explanations and suggestions about the Discussion, e.g. "hence, future research should seek to corroborate the findings or should try to answer this open question by avoiding the error of doing X..." The Discussion must communicate what went wrong in the research and what could be done better if one repeated the research and its write-up. Recommendations for future research must be provided in the Conclusions. Often these suggestions will be based upon what went wrong in the research as well as the implications of the overall findings for the product, service or concept.

Students should not include details of the results of their research but instead make reference to these as they were presented in the results section. The Discussion, as is true of the whole research project, should not advocate for the brand, concept, product, etc. that they have researched but should maintain a neutral and evaluative stance. Thus, company advertising and promotional material should be kept to a minimum. The Discussion/Conclusion is an extremely important section of the report and whether the discussion and conclusion are written as a single section or as two sections together, they should be approximately five to seven pages in length.

References/Bibliography/Reading List

All sources of literature (printed, online, and other media) cited during the research and its write-up should be included in the *references* using a consistent and recognized format of referencing (e.g., APA, Harvard, etc.). Background media and literature that influenced the research should be listed in a *bibliography* and suggested further reading should be included in the same format in a *reading list*.

Appendices

All research reports must include Appendices. In this section students will include all raw research data. For example, they should include copies of the transcripts of interviews, etc., along with photographs of sort and mapping procedures, etc. They should also include blank copies of the research instruments (interview schedules, blank mind-maps, etc.) and instructions that were given to respondents. If standardized verbal instructions were given then these must be typed-out and included.

Also incorporate any forms of background information about the product, service, concept, company, distributors, etc. that provide your readers with a better understanding of the results. This information is positioned in the Appendices if by inclusion in the main body of the research report the details distract readers from the research and its results or makes the document too difficult to read. All materials included in the Appendices should be in their own numbered or alphabetized appendix and there should be "call-outs/references" in the main body of the text that refers to each appendix.

There is no specific length to the appendices section.

Delivering the Written Research Report

Each team must present one written report per-team. This should be in digital format and **not** a printed document. **Printed accounts waste resources.** Digital reports may contain colour images, etc., and hyperlinks to guide the reader around the report in a way that printed matter cannot.

The final document must be submitted by the date and time given in the syllabus.

Verbal Research Presentation

Each team will present their research to the rest of the class using Power-Point/Keynote/Acrobat, etc. The presentation should be similar in format to a commercially commissioned market research project delivered to clients. Teams should become over-familiar with the contents of their presentation. This is for two reasons, 1/ so that presenters do not stumble over what they are introducing (if possible, team members should learn their part of the presentation and not read from notes), 2/ so that presenters can answer any questions that attending students and faculty members may ask.

Research teams should actively involve audience participation by giving the audience activities to do or questions to answer at appropriate points in the presentation.

Each team's presentation will be approximately 20–30 minutes in length **(the precise length of the team presentation will be announced in class).**

Following the presentation, the team should actively seek questions from the audience and attempt to answer these. The portion of an individual student's grade that reflects his or her contribution to the team project and presentation will be based on the quality of the final report, the presentation, and individual participation in the project. Group members will not necessarily receive the same grade.

4/ Individual Poster Presentation

Basic details

The individual poster presentation is the culmination of individual student learning during the semester and takes place at the end of the course. The bare bones of this assessment can be stated as a series of answers to questions:

Question 1: What do you have to do?
Answer1:   create a virtual poster

Question 2: What should this be about?
Answer 2:   a product, service or concept that you have not previously investigated or presented in your article review and hypothetical research design

Question 3: What format should this take?
Answer 3:   a single PowerPoint slide

Question 4: What do I do with this?
Answer 4:   present this to the class

Question 5: How long should the presentation be?
Answer 5:   6 minutes Each student will once again design a **hypothetical** *qualitative research project around a product, service, or concept that they want to investigate. The product, service, or concept teams choose for this presentation must be* **different** *from the product, service, or concept in the team research project and from the product, service or concept teams designed a hypothetical study around and presented at the end of your article presentation/evaluation.*

Further details

Students design a study addressing this new product or service that uses three or more of the research methods that they have encountered in this course.

For each research method that they use to investigate their product, service, or concept, teams must:

1/ Provide details of the sample of respondents they would ideally select to conduct the research
2/ Specify any research materials, locations, etc., that they will need for each of their three research procedures
3/ State the timescale for conducting this research project with the three procedures
4/ State the timescale for the entire research project (all three procedures together)
5/ Suggest what the results from each of the research approaches are likely to show and what these results are not likely to show in the project they are proposing
6/ Make very specific comments about each method and what each procedure may indicate about their product or service rather than general comments about the method in general

Students may decide to present three research methods that they think are well suited to investigate the chosen product or service. Alternatively, they may select methods that are not well suited to the specific product or service. Their other alternative is to present a selection of appropriate and inappropriate procedures. In all cases they must state the strengths and weaknesses of each of the three approaches and explain their positive and negative aspects in relation to investigating your topic of interest.

The poster that students present must demonstrate what they have learned from participating both in the team research project and in this course in qualitative consumer research in general. The poster must also describe the tangible benefits their research will provide to the product/service.

Poster details

1/ The poster must be a single PowerPoint /Keynote slide (or similar)
2/ Someone looking at the slide should be able to read this from approximately two meters (six feet)
3/ The poster should contain all of the details of the research project in brief (bulleted) form
4/ The poster should be visually attractive so as to engage viewers
5/ The poster should contain communicative graphics as necessary to clearly convey the research findings

Presentation details

The presentation students give must be approximately six minutes in length. They must rehearse their poster presentation to ensure their presentation is near the requisite six-minute time limit. Students' grades will be penalized if their presentation is one-minute more or less than six minutes.

The poster presentation must be on one single slide – it cannot be a multiple slide presentation. If students use multiple slides their grade will be penalized. Slides may not take the form of a Prezi or move in any way. The only exception to this is that they may introduce elements to their slide by clicking as they talk but all elements, once revealed, must remain visible on the slide until the end of the presentation.

In students' verbal presentation they must add details to the basic elements of their research project that are represented on the poster. They should not simply read the content of the poster. The poster and the verbal presentation should compliment each other and together provide more information than either the slide or the verbal presentation provides on its own.

Students must structure both their poster and their verbal presentation in a way that comprehensively sets forth their research.

To achieve a good grade it is important that students make their poster and presentation interesting. This is the culmination of their learning from the semester of classes and should demonstrate both the breadth and the specificity of their understanding. Therefore, students should not merely present the three approaches but indicate the greater depth of their knowledge. Part of demonstrating understanding may include explaining why they chose the particular approaches and why they rejected others.

Appendix B. Sample Course Schedule

Lecture	Material Covered	Activities
1	What is qualitative research/ethnography; Research approaches; What makes a good project	Decide team membership; Develop project ideas; Read about project area
2	Finalize projects; Research cycle, ethics, research methods, philosophies, approaches	Prepare presentation of your project
3	Ethics; Establishing clear research objectives, mapping sentences	Present project; Start ethics training - complete this by lecture 10
4	Research writing & reading	Continue ethics training
5	Project planning/design/recruitment	Develop sort item ideas
6	Sort approaches; Develop items for sort approach	Start article presentations; Revision for vignette
7	Assessment 1; Sort item development	Vignettes; Project proposal
8	Sort procedure – in-class workshop	Ethics training; Sort items for class; Analyse sort data
9	Focus group interview theory – benefits/problems	Develop focus group interview schedule
10	Focus group interview – develop in class	Complete/submit ethics certificate
11	Focus group interview – in-class workshop	Focus group interview schedule for class; Analyse focus group interview data
12	Attitude assessment, idea generation	Continue writing-up findings
13	In-depth interviews – discussion; Develop schedule in class for in-depth interviews	Develop in-depth interviews schedule
14	In-depth interviews – in-class workshop	In-depth interviews questions
15	In-depth interviews – optional in-class workshop; Discuss netnography /ethnography	Analyse in-depth interview data
16	Netnography/ethnography/observation – discussion	Out of class ethnography; Develop netnography
17	Netnography/ethnography/observation – in-class workshop	Netnography for class; Analyse netnography
18	Archival materials/Artefact; Visual Ethnography	Develop archival/artefact/visual materials
19	Archival materials/Artefact; Visual Ethnography: in-class workshop	Visual Ethnography for class; Analyse visual/archival/artefact materials
20	Life history, journals, diaries – when to use/benefits/problems	Develop journal
21	Life history, Journals, in-class workshop	Journal for class; Run Journal; Analyse visual/artefact/etc
22	Data analysis; Reporting findings,	Discussion
23	Effective presentations	Finalize write-up
24	In-class workshop	Results section due; Develop presentations
25	Individual presentations	Individual poster due
26	Individual presentations	
27	Group presentations	Group project due

Appendix C. Corresponding Readings from Qualitative Research Methods in Consumer Psychology: Ethnography and Culture *(Hackett, 2015, Routledge)*

Number and Title of Chapter in this Guide Book		Chapter Number in Qualitative Research Methods in Consumer Psychology: Ethnography and Culture
Chapter 2	Using a Mapping Sentence to Manage a Consumer Research Project	Chapter 1
Chapter 3	Research Ethics	Chapter 2
Chapter 4	Projective Techniques	Chapter 10
Chapter 5	Focus Groups	Chapters 7, 9
Chapter 6	In-Depth Interviews	Chapters 11, 12
Chapter 7	Ethnography	Chapters 6, 7, 13, 14
Chapter 8.	Netnography	Chapter 18
Chapter 9.	Visual Ethnography	Chapter 16
Chapter 10	Artefacts	Chapter 15
Chapter 11	Archives	Chapter 15
Chapter 12	Journals and Diaries	Chapter 17
Chapter 13	Autoethnography	Chapter 8
Chapter 14	Projective Techniques	Chapter 10
Chapter 15	Focus Groups	Chapters 7, 9
Chapter 16	In-Depth Interviews	Chapters 11, 12
Chapter 17	Ethnography	Chapters 6, 7, 13, 14
Chapter 18	Netnography	Chapter 18
Chapter 19	Visual Ethnography	Chapter 16
Chapter 20	Artefacts	Chapter 15
Chapter 21	Archives	Chapter 15
Chapter 22	Journals and Diaries	Chapter 17
Chapter 23	Autoethnography	Chapter 8

Index

165

Study Guides in Adult Education
Book Series

Simona Sava

Needs Analysis and Programme Planning in Adult Education

2012. 163 pp. Pb.
18,90 € (D), 19,50 € (A),
US$26.95, GBP 16.95
ISBN 978-3-86649-481-7

Book Series:

Cohen-Scali (ed.): Competence and Competence Development
Pätzold, Henning: Learning and Teaching in Adult Education
Lima/ Guimarães: European Strategies in Lifelong Learning
Bélanger, Paul: Theories in Adult Learning and Education
Oliver, Esther: Research and Development in Adult Education

Order now:

Barbara Budrich Publishers
Stauffenbergstr. 7, 51379 Leverkusen-Opladen
ph +49 (0)2171.344.594 fx +49 (0)2171.344.693
info@barbara-budrich.net

www.barbara-budrich.net

CPSIA information can be obtained at www.ICGtesting.com
Printed in the USA
LVOW10s0842280916

506531LV00008B/21/P

9 783847 407720